Is the Baw Burst?

A Long-Suffering Supporter's Search

for the Soul of Scottish Football

IAIN HYSLOP

Luath Press Limited

EDINBURGH

www.luath.co.uk

First published 2012

ISBN: 978-1-908373-22-9

Printed and bound by CPI Antony Rowe, Chippenham

Typeset in 11 point Sabon

To my wife, mum (we all still miss you very much), and the rest of family.

IAIN HYSLOP was born in Glasgow and now lives in Ayrshire. He served an apprenticeship in the Clyde shipyards and currently works in health and safety. He is a graduate of the Open University and Strathclyde University. A lifelong Scotland fan, he has followed the national team at home and abroad and is hoping the next big trip will be Brazil 2014. See you all there!

Contents

Acknowledgements

A big thank you to everyone at Luath Press who are a very friendly, helpful and knowledgeable group of people. Special thanks to Jennie for her gracious assertiveness that was essential in pulling everything together.

Thanks to Paul Martin for giving me an insight into life at the Rovers, to family and friends who assisted and encouraged me to write up my musings, and to my wife Debbi for putting up with all of this for the past two years. I am looking forward to much more time together.

Introduction

Welcome to *Is The Baw Burst?* This is a journey through Scottish football – the unofficial review. Yes, we've had the official one, in two parts, compiled by former First Minister Henry McLeish. This one is less formal, compiled by a football fan. Firstly, there was the fieldwork, 44 games attended in one season. The findings were analysed and the review developed with further research, scrutiny and comment on the dynamic, ever-changing Scottish football scene – there's a lot to discuss.

The catalyst was the official review, which I read whilst on holiday in Florida (anything to avoid another theme park). In my opinion, it missed some key points, particularly relating to the supporters who are the lifeblood of the game. McLeish set out to look at the state of the game from grassroots to professional level. And yes, he produced a fairly comprehensive review, much of which I agree with. He reported on youth development, facilities and resources, analysed the way players are nurtured, examined coaching techniques and football structures. He tried to bring all the elements together and see how the relationships worked or didn't work.

But the official report left me asking, what about the guys that go to the games every week? What's it like for us? What changes do we want? And so I decided to have a look for myself and find out if the baw was really burst.

I'd always wanted to go round every stadium in Scotland, so now was the time to go for it as I could think of no better way to get a feel for the game in this country. When I was a wee boy, I'd always watch the Saturday afternoon football shows on TV. I'd sit mesmerised as the scores came in listing teams from places like Forfar and Stenhousemuir that seemed strange and distant, not to mention the mysterious Queen of the South. 'Where are Morton and Clyde?' I would wonder. 'Are these Rovers from Albion a football team or a type of car?'

My journey through Scottish football took me to all the senior grounds. I visited every club side in the four top divisions in Scotland, attended one Champions League match at Old Trafford and watched Scotland versus world champions Spain at Hampden. Over 7,500 miles were travelled, 43 programmes purchased and 40 steak pies devoured – usually washed down with a Bovril. Nearly £700 was laid out on match tickets. Add petrol and other incidentals and the total cost exceeded £2,500.

I watched the games with another 310,791 supporters (216,746 being at just four games – Celtic Park, Ibrox, Hampden and Old Trafford). Hampden was visited twice (Queen's Park and Scotland) as was Ochilview, due to the ground-sharing arrangement between Stenhousemuir and East Stirlingshire.

I had intended to visit as many grounds as I could for the typical Saturday 3pm kick off and calculated this as a possibility over the course of a season. I knew it would be a tight schedule and other factors, including postponements, weather and personal commitments had an impact, so it turned out that many of the matches I attended were midweek and on Sundays. That made for an even broader review.

At every game I took notes, photographs and recordings on my iPhone. I usually travelled by car and more often than not, alone. Four of the games involved an overnight stay and some weekends I attended two games. Towards the end of the season I usually had a midweek fixture to attend due to postponements caused by weather conditions – winter 2010/11 is one of the worst I can remember and it completely changed my perspective on when we should play football in this country.

I tried to get as good a feel for each stadium as possible. I listened to football shows on the radio going to and from the games, read the programmes and tried to complete my notes as soon as possible after a match.

Some of my conclusions were reached pretty quickly while others developed over time. I have aimed for an impartial perspective of the game in Scotland. My questions and recommendations express my own thoughts and often they reflect the strongly-held views of the majority of my fellow Scottish football supporters. Some are controversial. All are worth thought and debate.

Despite the ongoing talk about league reconstruction and other possible changes, things have remained the same for far too long. Season 2011/12 began in customary fashion with numerous early exits from European tournaments; Scotland failed to qualify for the European Championships – business as usual. And then, early in February 2012, Rangers FC went into administration; the fans are outraged – the so-called leaders have let us down again. It is thought that the fans' season ticket money for the next four years has been used to clear legacy debt. The club face being barred from European competitions for some time and, as I write, the SFA have announced a year-long embargo on Rangers buying new players; add to the mix the likely outcome that Celtic will have a stranglehold on the game in this country for years to come, and it all makes for grim reading, not only for Rangers fans but for the chasing pack as well. The media feeding frenzy continues unabated. There is general disbelief that it could have got this bad for Rangers and for the Scottish game. Yet the warning signs have been around for years, just ask the fans of Dundee, Motherwell, Livingston – and Gretna, remember them? Look south to Portsmouth and Port Vale. Is it really that much of a shock? Anyway, we are where we are – the talking continues and season 2011/12 will be remembered for all the wrong reasons.

I decided to head along to Ibrox for the first game played after the club went into the hands of the administrators. Last time I experienced an 'administration' game was at Dens Park which was genuinely quite humbling. The fans are always at the crux of these matters and Rangers versus Kilmarnock was no different. At Ibrox the house was full and the talking continued long into the evening. Very little was football-related – it was all business, finance and blame.

One thing is for sure – football has to wake up to reality and get its house in order. Brave decisions must be taken and followed through. Surely this warning cannot be ignored. Huge changes are needed.

Financial problems, falling attendances, poor quality football, crumbling stadiums, terrible catering... is the picture really as bad as it's painted? Time to have a look. My review starts at Somerset Park and finishes at the Caledonian Stadium. I travelled through one of the worst winters in living memory, ate dodgy pies and listened to stories of death threats and bullets in the post. Along the way I encountered the world champions, the blue Brazil, 'lesser' Firs Park and an eerily empty Hampden, populated only by a few hundred Spiders. I've recorded arguments aplenty, cheeky comments and thumbnail match reports.

Things were gloomy back in August 2010 when this journey started. Issues like the credit crunch, annual failures on the European stage and the seemingly ever more prosperous English leagues were having an impact on Scottish football. Interest was waning and the fans were grumbling. The SFA were under increasing pressure to update its antiquated articles of association and conflict between the three organisations controlling the game (SFA, SPL and SFL) was commonplace. Supporters were crying out for league reconstruction, better representation at the clubs and more say in the overall running of the game – deep-rooted problems.

The research has continued ever since. A notable highlight was a chance meeting at Luton Airport with the Albion Rovers Manager Paul Martin. He gave me an invaluable insight into the game in the lower leagues. Further meetings and conversations revealed much about the struggles that these clubs face on a day-to-day basis. In fact, it's so far removed from the glamorous product shown constantly on TV, you could be forgiven for thinking it's a different sport – but that is the reality of the game in Scotland.

There is hope though, and it's worth noting that there is much going on behind the scenes. The youth set-ups and academies are a real shining light, the women's game is thriving and the national side is full of promising young players.

I learned a lot about the game in this country and have substance to back up my arguments. This book is for every football fan in the country to read and enjoy – and decide if the baw is burst or not. Game on!

THE HONEST MEN V THE CITY

Here We Go, Here We Go, Here We Go!

SATURDAY 7 AUGUST 2010, decision day. I had been thinking about this moment for months – with good reason, as this project was going to take up most of my free time for the next year or two and place unknown strains on my life.

But first of all the morning was busy with my usual Saturday stuff – cycling to Troon and back, a visit to the baker's for rolls and cakes, breakfast, reading papers, dog walking and betting – Saturday is definitely my favourite day of the week. Around 11.30 I decided to go for it and head along to Somerset Park for the 3 o'clock kick off. Suddenly I was tingling with anticipation at the prospect of starting my review of the state of Scottish football, and a visit to every stadium in the country – in what I hoped would turn out to be one of the great adventures of my life.

A quick Google search revealed that the ground was 2.3 miles from my Prestwick home. I hopped onto a No. 14 bus, disembarked just before 'Tam's Brig' and set off towards the old-fashioned floodlights, a sight once commonplace in Scotland's towns and cities.

My career as a football supporter has generally been as an afficionado of the big games, Ibrox, Hampden and Parkhead being my most common destinations, as well as some of the more famous stadiums in England and Europe. Over the years I have visited a number of smaller grounds as well, but for someone who particularly relishes Old Firm and Champions League games, walking up to Somerset Park that day was a very quiet affair. In front of me on McCall's Avenue were a dad and two boys; behind me was the loner with the Ayr United scarf who'd been on the bus. Not exactly a mass of people heading for the ground on the opening day of the season. Still, it was too early to pass judgement. I had to go with the flow and take in as much as possible.

First impressions are important. I had to look twice as I passed a turnstile section and a hospitality car park. Both areas looked like derelict factory entrances choked with weeds and rubbish. As I progressed towards the main entrance the situation was depressingly similar. My gloom was interrupted by a young vendor who presented me with the day's official match programme. He hurriedly gave me £2 change from a fiver (I later realised that he should have given me £3 change). There were a few people hanging around outside the main doorway, the club shop and at the entrances to the turnstiles marked 'Season Tickets Holders'. I wandered around for a while, taking some photographs and trying to fathom the attraction of coming to a place like this on my precious Saturday.

Too much thinking, just get in and see what's on offer, I told myself. I chose an empty turnstile to the left of the main door, walked straight in and handed over £20. The woman behind the grille smiled and swiftly produced a fiver from her money pouch. I didn't ask for a receipt or ticket and neither were forthcoming, so I clicked my way through the gate and into Somerset Park for the first time since the '70s. During one of our annual family summer sorties to our caravan at Croy Bay, my dad had met up with a work colleague who was an 'Honest Man' and they'd taken me along to an incredible match against Celtic. If my memory serves me correctly (I can't find the result online), Ayr United won 3-2. I got a bag of chips, the old man had a couple of pints with his mate and then we headed back along the coast road to continue our holiday – fantastic.

As I climbed up the stairs, I could see that Somerset Park had changed very little in 30-odd years since my last visit. I paused to get my bearings, located the toilets and the pie stall, and then headed out into the Main Stand. The beautifully manicured pitch was bathed in sunshine. Players from both teams were doing their warm-up exercises – as was the PA announcer, who was waxing lyrical about various promotions associated with the local community and the club. I made for the back row, sat down and took in the antiquated surroundings – Somerset Park stadium is definitely on its last legs.

The surrounding seats slowly filled with diehards, a blind chap and players from the Brechin City squad. Ayr United legend Henry Templeton took a seat right in front of me. Bunting tape separated the

We Are Hibernian: The Fans' Story

Andy MacVannan

ISBN 978 1906817 99 2 HBK £14.99

We are Hibernian explores the sights, sounds and memories of fans who have taken the 'journey' to watch the team that they love. Supporters from all walks of life bare their souls with humour, emotion and sincerity.

This book celebrates the story behind that unforgettable moment when Hibernian entered the childhood of its fans' lives and why, despite their different backgrounds, these loyal fans still support a sometimes unsupportable cause together.

Is it what happens on the field of play or the binding of tradition, memories and experience that makes Hibs fans follow their team through thick and thin? Featuring interviews with many different fans, this book takes you on a journey to discover why football is more than just a game and why Hibernian is woven into the DNA of each and every one of its supporters.

Everyone walked out that ground like they had just seen the second coming.
IRVINE WELSH, WRITER

My family were Irish immigrants. My father had renounced his Catholicism but had retained a blind faith in Hibs.
LORD MARTIN O'NEILL, POLITICIAN

In the early 1950s Alan, Dougie and I caught the tail end of the legendary Hibs team when they were still the best team in the world.
BRUCE FINDLAY, MUSIC BUSINESS MANAGER

Hibernian: From Joe Baker to Turnbull's Tornadoes

Tom Wright

ISBN 978 1908873 09 1 HBK £20

In Hibernian: From Joe Baker to Turnbull's Tornadoes, club historian Tom Wright marks a new dawn for the game and the end of an era for Hibs.

Hibernian begins in the turbulent 1960s, when relegation was avoided at Easter Road on the final day of the 1963 season.

The appointment of the legendary manager Jock Stein in 1964 saw an immediate improvement in the relegation haunted side. The Hibs side of the mid-'60s featured an all-Scottish international forward line, and the return of player Eddie Turnbull in 1971 saw the emergence of possibly Hibs' greatest-ever side – the magical Turnbull's Tornadoes.

Packed full of detail and interesting information, Hibernian is a must not only for Hibs supporters, but also for the general football fan who is interested in this defining period in the history of our game.

Luath Press Limited

committed to publishing well written books worth reading

LUATH PRESS takes its name from Robert Burns, whose little collie Luath (*Gael.*, swift or nimble) tripped up Jean Armour at a wedding and gave him the chance to speak to the woman who was to be his wife and the abiding love of his life. Burns called one of the 'Twa Dogs' Luath after Cuchullin's hunting dog in Ossian's *Fingal*. Luath Press was established in 1981 in the heart of Burns country, and is now based a few steps up the road from Burns' first lodgings on Edinburgh's Royal Mile. Luath offers you distinctive writing with a hint of unexpected pleasures.

Most bookshops in the UK, the US, Canada, Australia, New Zealand and parts of Europe, either carry our books in stock or can order them for you. To order direct from us, please send a £sterling cheque, postal order, international money order or your credit card details (number, address of cardholder and expiry date) to us at the address below. Please add post and packing as follows: UK – £1.00 per delivery address; overseas surface mail – £2.50 per delivery address; overseas airmail – £3.50 for the first book to each delivery address, plus £1.00 for each additional book by airmail to the same address. If your order is a gift, we will happily enclose your card or message at no extra charge.

Luath Press Limited

543/2 Castlehill
The Royal Mile
Edinburgh EH1 2ND
Scotland
Telephone: +44 (0)131 225 4326
(24 hours)
Fax: +44 (0)131 225 4324
email: sales@luath. co.uk
Website: www. luath.co.uk

100 or so away support from the rest, a couple of eagle-eyed stewards presiding over the segregation measures. Moderate applause greeted the teams as they ran out onto the sun-kissed turf; another SFL season was about to begin.

The game was lively enough, considering it was the first of the season. Brechin always tried to play football, which was refreshing. As for Ayr, not much to shout about for a team that had played at a higher level the previous year – there certainly wasn't a division of a difference between the teams. The game passed quickly and at the half-time whistle I set off to sample some of the local produce. The courteous staff, beavering away in their dilapidated hidey-hole, were seemingly oblivious to their surroundings. I thought back to my recent trip to America and the glaring differences at point of sale. However, steak pie and Bovril purchased, I returned to my seat, devoured my tasty snack and readied myself for the second period.

The second half was enjoyable and the home support even managed a song midway through. One or two players were really starting to stand out and were dictating just about every aspect. Others looked to be tiring but the game remained interesting until the final whistle ended it, drawing groans from the home support and lots of cheering from the far travelled 'City' fans.

A lot to think about as I retraced my steps back to the bus stop. Had I enjoyed my experience enough to come here again? Would children and teenagers enjoy an afternoon at Somerset Park? What did

The sun always shines at Somerset

the future hold for Ayr United? I decided to hone my thoughts over a few beers and got off the bus at the stop nearest to the Central Bar in Prestwick... 'Pint of Tennent's, please.'

In a town with a population of nearly 50,000 you would expect a healthier support than 1,212 at the start of a season – particularly given that Kilmarnock, the nearest senior club and main rival to Ayr United, is a good 15 miles away. Surely Ayr United, located as it is in football mad Ayrshire, should be the pinnacle of football, at least for South Ayrshire. Every local boy and girl should dream of pulling on the colours and walking out in front of friends and family.

Unfortunately for Ayr, Ayr United and the surrounding area, the Somerset Park environment is not very appealing. Where's the inspiration in an old stadium surrounded by derelict buildings and railway lines. Is it the type of place you would want your kids to go along to? The stadium seems stuck in a time warp, waiting for someone to turn the lights off for good.

But does that have to be the shape of things to come? Just along the road at Craigie is the new £70 million Ayr Campus of the University of the West of Scotland. It was still under construction at the time of my visit to Somerset Park and opened in August 2011. It has excellent transport links to the town centre and major road networks. You would think that someone would have recognised this as an ideal opportunity to put the club at the heart of the local community by involving the football club in the development and investigating the possibilities of shared usage of sports facilities and the potential for exploring business opportunities. Surely the Ayr United Football Academy (which is a real shining light for the club) would benefit from this kind of infrastructure.

But we are where we are and the fans will need to put up with Somerset for the foreseeable future. The Academy set-up is encouraging though. This looks like the way forward for clubs and communities alike. The stakeholders include NHS, South Ayrshire Council, Ayr College and the football club. The initiatives are all centred on using football to improve the lives and health of the people in South Ayrshire and this will hopefully benefit the club long term as well. The downside is that the soccer scholarships are based in the USA – it would be great if we could offer them here in Scotland.

My first impressions of Ayr United weren't favourable, primarily due to Somerset Park. It would be so nice to go for a walk along the River Ayr and then head into a modern arena to enjoy some refreshments and watch the football. The evident lack of investment in the stadium over the years is short-sighted, not to mention disrespectful to the fans. However, the focus on the Academy is encouraging and, importantly, the whole community stands to benefit from that.

Quote of the day – *The Wife: 'Has it went to extra time?'*

GAME	AYR UNITED VERSUS BRECHIN CITY
DIVISION	SFL 2
DATE	SAT 7 AUGUST 2010, KO 3PM
VENUE	SOMERSET PARK, ATTENDANCE 1,212
SCORE	0-2

MATCH STATS:
HTTP://WWW.SCOTTISHFOOTBALLLEAGUE.COM/FOOTBALL/SECOND/RESULTS/3285841/

2

THE STEELMEN V THE HIBEES

All is Not Well with the Pies

ANOTHER LOVELY DAY, perfect for the beach or other outdoor activities. But there I was, heading up the M77 for Motherwell and a taste of SPL action. Today's midday kick off was something I had experienced on only a couple of occasions before as a supporter and as an armchair fan (or bar stool fan, to be precise) and I didn't find it particularly appealing. Today was different. For one thing there would be no alcohol involved as I was driving and also suffering a touch from the previous day's excesses at a wedding at Ayr Racecourse. I fully intended to choose 3pm Saturday games wherever possible but with a tight schedule to adhere to over the season, the inclusion of a couple of Sunday games and some midweek fixtures would be necessary but would also broaden the scope of the review.

About an hour later, I parked on George Street. I turned left onto Manse Road and headed towards the sets of floodlights similar to the ones at Somerset Park. I had frequented Fir Park on and off over the years as an old friend was a Well supporter and he used to drag me along. I was present at the now famous 1991 Scottish Cup Final victory over Dundee United at Hampden, stuff of legend for a small provincial club like Motherwell. It had been a few years since I'd been back. I was looking forward to seeing the young Motherwell team. They had had a wonderful 2009/10 season, successfully securing a European place and – more importantly – flying the flag by negotiating the qualifying rounds so far, a feat that neither Celtic or Hibs managed in their respective competitions this week. 'Mon the Well!

The residential streets were strangely quiet until the junction of Manse Road and Edward Street. From this point onwards it started to feel more like going to a football match. I carried on up past the Fir Park Social Club and towards the ticket office nestled between the

Davie Cooper and Phil O'Donnell stands, which almost touch, two names from opposing sides of the Old Firm remembered here without any prejudice by the Steel Men. It was the first time I'd been at the ground since Phil's tragic death and I was pleased that they had named a stand after him. And Cooper, a traditional winger, had been an outrageously skilful footballer. The more I thought about it, the more I felt that we'd not seen the like since. Why we don't encourage, coach and nurture people to fulfil that role is a mystery to me.

I wandered round the stadium in amongst the home and away fans, then headed up towards the main road. The stadium is close to the town centre, which has good transport links, rail and motorway networks – the type of infrastructure you would expect in and around big towns. In terms of industry, few Scottish towns were bigger than Motherwell; in its heyday it was a real industrial powerhouse. What came first, the stadium or the houses and school and college buildings surrounding it? Probably the former, and therein lies one of the club's main problems. It would be difficult to expand or alter the facility in its present location unless there was some serious co-ordination with the adjacent educational establishments. Perhaps some sort of collaboration has been suggested and turned out not to be feasible, leaving the club to concentrate on what they've got. It would be so good, though, to see a load of training pitches and other sports and leisure facilities for the community, with the stadium as the jewel in the crown, but for the foreseeable future it looks as if the good people of Motherwell will have to put up with four ill-assorted stands, each completely different from the rest.

Twenty-five quid in hand, I went through under a sign displaying £22, which looked as though it had been overpainted recently, and up into the Phil O'Donnell Stand via the snack bar, where I paid £1.70 for a Coke. My chosen seat had no back and was to the rear of the stand. Behind me in the press gantry the hacks were already in place, laptops open and primed for action. The tannoy was blasting out pop music which was intermittently interrupted by offers of club merchandise – including seats on the club charter flight to Denmark. All very encouraging, but I couldn't help feeling that, considering their recent achievements, there should have been a better buzz about the place. Had the midday kick off put off some punters, I wondered, but not for long. The 5,000 plus attendance, announced during the game, was similar to the previous two seasons' average gates. I was experiencing a typical SPL game without any of the big two – so much quieter.

'Mon the Well

I thought back to the previous week's game and Ayr United in general. Motherwell has approximately 15,000 less of a population than Ayr, has more clubs close by that you could class as serious opposition and has suffered more than most in terms of manufacturing decline. Yet, when it comes to the beautiful game, the Steelmen are in much better shape than their coastal cousins. Why are Ayr United in such a lowly position?

A strange delay followed the ball being placed in the centre spot – one can only assume this was down to the live TV coverage and the referee awaiting a signal to proceed. Eventually we were off. The game was noticeably quicker than last week's Second Division encounter. The players looked taller, faster and, stating the obvious here, fitter due to their full-time status. The game was reasonably balanced in the first half. Motherwell were typically well organised with Hibs offering a touch more flair. One or two quality ball players make all the difference and Hibs had Miller and Riordan continually seeking to be creative. The half finished even at 1-1. Pie and Bovril time.

I joined a queue adjacent to the main staircase, which was also on the main passageway to the Gents. The queue was extremely slow moving and people were starting to get agitated. I reached the counter after about ten minutes and placed my order. The supervisor was busy piercing pies with a thermometer and relaying a 'not ready' message to the rest of the staff. Incredibly, they had no pies ready for the half-time rush and yet the staff lacked any urgency. Scotland completely bewilders me sometimes. After another couple of minutes, the pies reached the desired temperature and I purchased a Chapman's creation (nothing else on offer) and a Bovril, and hurried back to my pew. The pie was served on a small paper plate and as I lifted it to my mouth at a slight angle, a stream of grease engulfed the crotch area of my khaki-coloured trousers – wonderful. The pie was disgusting, most was discarded, but the Bovril was excellent. My experience so far, not including fuel, had cost £30 and I would now have a dry cleaning bill as well.

Second half under way, both teams going for it. At last, some banter from the fans. The Hibees lot had more to shout about after another couple of good goals hit the back of the Well net. The managers introduced a few subs, the referee made some dodgy decisions, Motherwell got a penalty and the match was by and large exciting up to the final whistle. The Motherwell fans, a good mixture of young and old, male and female, had started leaving before the end and this seemed to contribute to the noise the few hundred Hibees were making. Game over.

As I drove home I recalled former Motherwell manager Terry Butcher complaining of a general lack of facilities. I'm assuming he meant indoor facilities, as there is an abundance of outdoor stuff in Strathclyde Park which is nearby. Henry McLeish's official review of Scottish football highlights many shortfalls in this respect. But as there are many facilities available, particularly in schools and colleges, it seems to me that the problem lies primarily with accessibility. Having said that, I'm not altogether convinced that quality facilities alone would, of themselves, transform the game – did we have any 'quality facilities' in the '50s and '60s?

What would improve the game throughout Scotland is more interaction with the fans and local communities. Like Ayr United, the Steelmen have a strong presence in the local community with various initiatives such as Soccer Schools, health and wellbeing guidance and lifelong learning. Another interesting development is the recently established Well Society, created using shares donated by the former Chairman, John Boyle. This bold scheme aims to empower the fans and to ensure that, among other things, the club is run as a community asset, grows sustainably and plays at the highest levels possible without the risk of administration. There are varying levels of membership – all the information is available online. James McFadden, one of several former player helping to promote the scheme, tell fans: 'You can help secure the future of the club by joining up now. It's your opportunity to have a say in how our club is run.'

All very encouraging – the club trying to grow organically within the locale and bring everyone else along with them. The constraints of the stadium could be overcome through building more liaisons with the neighbours. Where there's a will, there's a way.

Quote of the day – *The wife: 'Why haven't you ticked all the boxes beside the squad lists on the back of the programme?' There's only 11 in each team, darling!*

GAME	MOTHERWELL VERSUS HIBS
DIVISION	PREMIER
DATE	SUN 15 AUGUST 2010, KO 12PM
VENUE	FIR PARK, ATTENDANCE 5,172
SCORE	2-3

MATCH STATS:
HTTP://WWW.SCOTPREM.COM/CONTENT/DEFAULT.ASP?PAGE=S27_1_1
&WORKINGDATE=2010-8-15

3

THE BULLY WEE V THE BORDERERS

The Flow Must Go On

CONFUSION REIGNED IN the Hyslop household. Youngest boy, an 11-month-old Tibetan terrier, was getting his haircut and wasn't due out of the clippers until 1.15, seriously curtailing my options of making a game. Compounding the situation, I had foolishly said to my wife that I could drop her at her my sister's – if, and only and if, I decided to go to Broadwood and take in Clyde v Berwick Rangers. My other option, Morton, disappeared when the clipper announced that the pup would not be ready until after one, so the decision was that the Bully Wee would have an extra spectator. It's no' easy getting to the football every week.

At 2.50 I pulled up in front of Broadwood to enquire about the parking arrangements and a young steward gave me a comprehensive set of directions to the away car park. I could have done with the shorter version. Despite my concerns about being late, within five minutes I was parked and walking towards the Main Stand (the other two were closed and where the fourth stand should be was a leisure centre). I purchased a programme (excellent quality and value), tried to go in a turnstile at the 'Berwick end' but was directed away by a steward who somehow knew I wasn't from south of the border. I then tried to go in through the 'accompanied persons' section before being directed to the 'adults only' opening where I paid my £10 and noisily clicked through the revolving bars and into the stadium for the first time in over five years.

I thought back to my first game here. The great Manchester United had been the visitors with Giggs, Scholes, Rooney *et al* strutting their stuff and running out easy winners. However, I will always remember Clyde's performance that day. The bunch of trialists flung together by Graham Roberts and Joe Miller put up an incredible show against the premiership big boys, much to the delight of the Broadwood faithful. What a difference five years makes.

I climbed up a few flights of stairs, made my way along some passageways and emerged into the blustery air. The stand was busy enough, which certainly contributed to the atmosphere, although there were less than a thousand people in the ground – the lively mood was down to the one-stand arrangement. There were lots of grandads, dads and sons in the crowd, many of them munching on pies and hot dogs which looked very tasty.

There was an energetic start to the game. I'd been expecting plenty of goals in the lower league matches – the tactical battles that you get with the 'big boys' don't seem to materialise and the teams look to be going for a win, which is refreshing. None of this sitting back, soaking up the pressure, hoping to get a sneaky breakaway.

As the game raged on, I kept being distracted by the stewards. Not that they were annoying or anything. On the contrary, they were proficient, smartly dressed, courteous and hard-working, easily the most professional that I had come across for some time – I wondered if they were council employees? Overall, the set-up was very good and this impression was enhanced at half time by the swift service at the modern snack bar and ad hoc units selling hot dogs. Pie (steak) and Bovril, both good, were demolished quickly enough to allow time for a browse through the programme and it was good to see that there was involvement with local youth clubs. I   checked the rest of scores on the iPhone and then the game resumed. I was enjoying my day.

Unfortunately, the diehard Bully Wee fans were not. From Clyde's point of view, the equaliser that should have been built on just after half time was quickly eradicated from the minds of the faithful as Berwick took advantage of sloppy defending and rattled in another three goals. The game was over with about 20 minutes to go and the Bully Wee fans' criticism of the players was incessant. My awareness of this might have been down to the fact that everyone was housed in the same stand, and there could well have been more derogatory comments at the two other matches, particularly from the terraces, which used to be infamous for the more vociferous types. As the dejected Bully Wee fans started leaving the stand, the jubilant cries of the far-travelled away fans rose in volume. They, at least, were enjoying themselves, and all credit to them. The final whistle was met with a chorus of boos.

The route back to the car took me past numerous artificial pitches, all being used by local youths. This was encouraging, as not only were they playing football but many of them had evidently cycled there as well. I wondered how many people from the modern housing estates that surround the stadium actually came to support the team, and how this compared with years gone by when they played at Shawfield within a sprawl of tenement communities and pubs.

Exiting the car park was well managed with stewards on hand if required. It occurred to me that I had seen no police presence in or around the ground.

As I joined the flow of traffic heading towards Glasgow, I noticed numerous new housing estates and industrial units had sprung up close to the ground. I'm sure that the development of this new community will continue apace now that the A80 has finally been upgraded to motorway status. Will the football club be at the heart of this new community? That certainly should be the aim.

Henry McLeish's review identifies lack of facilities as a serious shortfall in Scottish football. For Clyde, the facilities look to be in place with potential for further development, and not many Scottish clubs have this luxury. The club's well-documented financial difficulties have contributed to its freefall through the divisions – good facilities alone will not preserve a club. Lack of quality on the park is also an issue here and this will not be an overnight fix. However, the infrastructure is in place, which is crucial, and seems to be developing, which is encouraging. Many other Scottish football clubs must be in envy of Clyde's set-up. That's why it's difficult to understand the talk of them leaving Broadwood – to go where? Rutherglen is the club's traditional

Broadwood – Home of the Bully Wee

heartland, and indeed the Southside Branch of the Clyde FC School of Football is based there, so it would seem an obvious choice; but unfortunately a purpose-built stadium is lacking, unlike here at Broadwood on the outskirts of Cumbernauld.

Interestingly, this old football club (established in 1877) is on a journey back to its humble beginnings. At the outset it was a sports club owned by the supporters and dedicated to the local community. Today, the Clyde Community Interest Club (Clyde CIC) is up and running and already a few hundred fans have joined. The CIC claim that the format is successful, citing the German Bundesliga as an example of how things could be. Powerhouse clubs such as Bayern Munich, Schalke and Eintracht Frankfurt have been using the one-member-one-vote system for years with outstanding success. There is no club in administration or burdened with crippling debt in the German top flight but there are full stadiums, cheap admission prices and regular European success. However, there is always a flip-side and Port Vale's recent disastrous slide into administration is a warning sign that can't be ignored; fans running clubs doesn't always work.

Clyde's efforts must be commended. If the club and the community can grow together, and if there is some joined-up thinking and planning, there is real hope of a renaissance for the Bully Wee.

Quote of the day – Clyde fan shouts to the manager: 'You've got to change this, Stuart!' He got an ironic look from the manager as he had no other options, he couldn't change it.

GAME	CLYDE VERSUS BERWICK RANGERS
DIVISION	SFL3
DATE	SAT 21 AUGUST 2010, KO 3PM
VENUE	BROADWOOD STADIUM, ATTENDANCE 772
SCORE	1-4

MATCH STATS:
HTTP://WWW.SCOTTISHFOOTBALLLEAGUE.COM/FOOTBALL/THIRD/
RESULTS/3285980/

4

THE SPIDERS V THE BORDERERS

The Spiders that Never Tried

USUAL SCENARIO: THE 3BS (bakers, breakfast and betting), dog walking and also a cycle along the path to the Marine Hotel in Troon for a swim and a shave. The early visit to the health club was unusual, but required, as I was planning on some beers with friends in Glasgow that evening. Pencilled in were a few potential games – Stirling v Dunfermline, Livingston v Forfar and Rangers v St Johnstone – the game at Ibrox being the most convenient for easy transfer back to the city centre by car. It occurred to me that it might be a different story on public transport and I didn't want to risk disrupting the lads' agenda, which would be under way from around 4.30. Back to the match schedule on the laptop. Nothing else in the SPL, Ayr and Clyde already visited, and SFL1 had nothing within the required timescales. I took another look at SFL3. Eureka! The Spiders were at Hampden. The national stadium it was (and probably would be for the next game as well – Scotland v Lichtenstein on Tuesday week).

I was intrigued by the thought of going to see Queen's Park. In my formative years we had lived in the shadow of Hampden in Curling Crescent, Kings Park. Had the Ol' Man taken me along to a game? I couldn't be sure but nothing sprang to mind... and by now the Ol' Yin would probably not remember anyway.

My wife duly informed of my intentions, we set off for Prestwick Station to catch the 1.19 to Glasgow Central. Wife and pups kissed goodbye, return ticket to Mount Florida purchased (for a very reasonable £8.75), *Daily Record* open at the football section, and I was all set. I've always enjoyed train rides up to Glasgow for the football, for a variety of reasons – the excitement, the anticipation, maintaining longstanding friendships and beer. The best ever was in 2007 for the Scotland v Italy game: a packed train bouncing all the way up the coast, excitement levels at fever pitch. Everyone believed we were going to beat the world champions (as we should have done) only to be utterly deflated a couple of minutes into the game when Luca Toni scored – and Scotland went silent.

The excitement levels for today's Third Division encounter were not quite in that league. Walking down Florida Street towards the ground, you wouldn't have known that there was a game on. This eerie feeling continued until I got close enough to see the cars parked near the big Hampden sign on Somerville Drive and heard smokers outside the Spiders members' club chatting together while enjoying a puff.

Turning right, I headed along in between the 'Rangers end' and lesser Hampden, stopping to take in the view of the artificial pitch and the wooden stand, which looks like it's been around since 1867 when this unique football club (still amateur) was formed, after 'a number of gentlemen met'. I carried on round towards the main entrance. There was a game on after all. People were arriving on foot and by car (although I've seen the car park fuller during normal weekdays) and entering through a couple of turnstiles in the South Stand. I parted with £11 for my ticket and walked into a Hampden atmosphere the likes of which I'd never before experienced. It was so quiet.

There was some activity around the Ladbrokes counter, which serves as the club shop on Queen's Park match days. I ambled around, looking at the wall-mounted pictures of the old ground bursting at the seams during big games, and portraits of Scotland players, past and present (some of the more recent ones I struggled to name, there's been that many of them). The fast food outlets were doing a steady trade. When there's an international match on, speed of service is poor at the half-time rush but they would probably cope today. The club shop was doing a brisk trade in programmes, memorabilia and draw tickets. It was in the charge of a fan clad in black and white who was clearly loving every minute of it. It's guys like him who are the lifeblood of the game, not only supporting their clubs but working for them as well – commitment without compromise.

Kick off fast approaching, I made my way out into the sunshine. The seating arrangements must have been unique in the national stadium, which has a capacity of around 50,000: there were only a couple of occupied sections, demarcated by bunting tape, a few stewards and four St Andrews first-aid personnel (almost one per supporter) looking on. There was surprisingly little in the way of pitch-side advertising and, as at Broadwood last week, no obvious police presence. And

Something missing?

very few fans. (Next day the crowd was reported to have been 497. It didn't even seem to be that many at the time.) They generated very little atmosphere, the noisiest part of the game being when the teams ran out to 'Two Tribes'. At least the pitch looked good.

There were no fireworks, national anthems or drunken singsongs before the game, just a few shouts, then the sprightly young men set about their business. I thought about my previous Hampden experiences; packed terraces, overflowing toilets – and back in 1976, sheer terror as the crowd surged forward towards the turnstiles at the Scottish Cup Final. We eventually turned back but I will always remember the madness of some of the supporters that day and their efforts to access the stadium: long-haired youths getting punted up over walls covered in barbed wire, some falling back into the throng, others getting ripped to shreds but continuing nevertheless. They must have been seriously drunk. The general lack of control was an obvious concern that has since been addressed by better stadiums, all-ticket matches and, perhaps most significantly, by the alcohol ban. (While I had no wish to return to those dark days, a pint would have gone down nicely.)

On the pitch both teams were trying to play football, there was virtually no play-acting and the players worked hard. On the other hand, there was a pretty lacklustre performance by the home support – they put me in mind of a quiet bunch of dudes sitting around a bowling green.

The QPFC flag blowing about in the wind above the North Stand stirred a memory – the corner flags used at international matches and cup finals used to have the same logo. With half time approaching, my thoughts turned to the prospect of food and as soon as the referee whistled I made a move and took my place third in line at the snack bar. The service was far quicker than I'd experienced before and everything I desired was available: steak pie, chips and Bovril. I consumed what turned out to be my evening meal, leaning against one of the shelves around the perimeter of the concourse, watching and listening to Spiders fans discussing the first half, checking results from other leagues and generally enjoying the ambience.

Berwick Rangers were the better team and during the second half, the game seemed to be a side issue for many of the home supporters, who blethered away about social events and the next couple of away games. In between nationalist shouts aimed at the fans who had crossed the border to support Berwick, there was some talk of the next qualifying games for Scotland. Incredibly, according to (some of) the fans who share the stadium with the national team, the campaign was as good as over before it had even begun. 'We'll never qualify, we're pish,' said one. He wasn't the only one writing off Scotland's chances before the tournament had even started. This negativity must be having a detrimental effect on our national game.

The world famous Hampden

Game over and another away victory. That's four out of four for the games I've attended so far this season and I've never bet on one of them. I had a last look around

Phenomenal at Lesser Hampden

the inside of the empty stadium and headed down the stairs. On the way up the hill to Mount Florida station, I couldn't help wondering what everyone was up to in the tenements and multi-storeys that surround the stadium. If a club struggles for support in a densely populated area like this, what chance do the rest of the teams have?

According to all accounts this is a great stadium to play in; it has indoor facilities, an all-weather pitch (Lesser Hampden) and, significantly, an indoor football centre just minutes along the road at Toryglen. However, it's crystal clear that facilities alone will not make Scotland a force in world football again. Facilities are merely a part of the picture. What needs addressing is the culture at the heart of the wider system. As a health and safety manager, my biggest professional challenge is to change the cultures that exist within industry. Who could argue that less deaths, injuries and illness are not a good thing? Yet every day people like myself are ridiculed for trying get this message across. It could be even harder in the realm of football.

As for Queen's Park, like their old rivals, Clyde, it would seem that certain parts of the system are healthier than others. There are some obvious shortfalls, particularly the virtually empty stadium for most home games despite such a busy locale. There are positives though, and these should be starting points from which to further develop the club, with its good sporting infrastructure playing a key part. Schools and businesses in the surrounding area should be considered as untapped resources both in terms of revenue and footballing skills. There is also a large ethnic community resident locally who might be encouraged to come along and enjoy an afternoon at Hampden. And, finally, why not play at lesser Hampden? Now I know many of the QP faithful will baulk at this suggestion. The national stadium is their traditional home and it adds a specialness to the club, and indeed to the occasion for the other teams when they visit. However, it's all a touch bizarre sitting in that huge arena with just a few hundred people around. A move to more intimate setting could help both the atmosphere and the team – worth a thought. All of these initiatives require sustained effort – it's the only way to move forward and protect important institutions like Queen's Park. Rant over – time for a beer.

Quote of the day – *Queen's Park fan talking about a St Andrew's First Aid woman: 'I hope she never needs to give me the kiss of life, that would be the end of me.'*

GAME	QUEEN'S PARK VERSUS BERWICK RANGERS
DIVISION	SFL3
DATE	SAT 28 AUGUST 2010, KO 3PM
VENUE	HAMPDEN, ATTENDANCE 479
SCORE	0-2

MATCH STATS:
HTTP://WWW.SCOTTISHFOOTBALLLEAGUE.COM/FOOTBALL/THIRD/
RESULTS/3286050/

5

THE BLUES V THE SPIDERS

Caravan Blues

WHAT A COUPLE OF WEEKS it's been. The negativity that I experienced at Hampden regarding the Scotland team reached fever pitch over the last few days and yet we are top of our Euro group. Don't get me wrong, there certainly wasn't a lot to shout about over the game in Lithuania and the encounter with Lichtenstein a few days later but we got four points and other results went our way. Everything considered, a reasonable start. However, it must have felt like the world was coming to an end for the Scottish players and management with howls of derision coming from every quarter, commentators claiming careers were over, calls for the manager to be sacked, phone-ins red hot with everybody and their granny having a kick at our game. This negativity is a deep-rooted problem that is undermining all that is good about our game and must cease if we are to progress.

I decided not to go to Hampden for the Lichtenstein game. One of the lads was looking for a ticket so, when I weighed up the pros and cons of a midweek fixture with one of the group minnows, I decided to let him have it. Anyway, I'm not keen on midweek fixtures, they always end up being a bit of a rush and the next day is usually a struggle. But, as I settled down on the couch with a beer and watched the teams run out, I felt a surge of regret. I've not missed a home match (friendlies apart) for years and it's amazing how you get used to being there, supporting the country you love, experiencing all the highs and lows. Tuesday's game was close to being the ultimate low, until seven minutes into injury time when McManus directed a cross ball into the back of the net. The Tartan Army were set to mobilise again in a few weeks with more than just a carry-out in the bag – there were four points in it as well.

Back to the 'real football' and there was a dilemma: Stranraer or

Annan? The wife – and pups – would be joining me on this leg of the journey and she was busy searching online for walks in the areas. I settled on Stranraer. Car loaded, we set off on another glorious day that could have been very productive in the garden.

An hour and a half later, after a splendid drive down the coast, Stranraer came into view. This was my first visit to Stair Park and I honestly had no idea what to expect. Having located the clearly signposted entrance, we drove back into town to find the tourist information centre, then headed back to the stadium. I was deposited outside the 'Coo Shed' and the wife headed off for a coastal walk, tourist leaflets in hand.

I was impressed by the surroundings of Stair Park: plenty of sports facilities, including grass and artificial pitches. There was ample parking adjacent to the stadium, both on tracks and on the football pitches. The stadium was easily accessible from the town centre and it had a good feel about it.

I wandered round to the reasonably new Main Stand (a Barr Construction Stadium) and had a quick look in the tiny club shop. Up the corridor you could see some players and officials enthusiastically going about their business. There was definitely a buzz about the place. I went back outside. By the main entrance two coaches were parked with one liveried with 'Marshall of Baillieston' – I couldn't work out why it had the Stranraer logo on the windows – might some fans travel from Glasgow's east end? I passed through the turnstile and into the stairwell, which was covered in pigeon droppings, climbed three flights of stairs, stopping at the top to try and locate the snack bar and toilets. Unfortunately for myself, the loyal supporters and the club, there was no snack bar to be found in the Main Stand. This service was provided by an adjacent 'caravan type' outlet. I carried on out into the sunshine and took a seat near the back of the stand.

I liked the stadium. There was a mixture of seats and terraces on three sides, all close to the pitch. The north side was a grass strip a couple of metres wide, tree-lined to the rear. You could almost stand on the touchline at some points and many took advantage of this by leaning on the breeze-block walls that demarcated the supporters from the on-field action. The place was beginning to fill up. As well as a fair few older people, there were lots of families and plenty of kids running around, annoying all the serious football folk. The stadium announcer indicated that the proceedings were about to get under way: 'Back to the real football,' he proclaimed, enjoying his side-swipe at the two

Where's the Stairs?

recent internationals. We were off.

Both the game and the supporters were lively throughout. There was plenty of action on the field and singing on the terraces and the game concluded with an injury-time winner for the home side, preceded by a sending-off for each team – great drama. The teams refreshingly avoided the nonsensical play-acting so frequent in the higher leagues. The banter between the two benches (The QP dugout had at one point 12 people in and around it, until the referee intervened) was jovial throughout and I enjoyed this aspect of the experience.

The catering, or lack of it, was the downside. The entire stadium seemed to be serviced by the one caravan outlet and this was totally inadequate. I queued up for the duration of half time, only to be informed that there was no hot food left apart from bacon rolls. I settled for a cup of Bovril, they settled for the 70 pence change I had in my hand rather than a £20 note. As I left the counter I felt sorry for the considerable number of people still in the queue.

Catering at football matches should be a no-brainer. You're guaranteed x amount of people every other week – why on earth can someone not work this out and make themselves a right good living at Stair Park? People will buy food at a game, it's part and parcel of the experience, so why not make sure both the quality and service are good? Get the basics right!

Lots to mull over. Shouldn't a town with a 13,000-plus population have a healthier interest in the events at Stair Park? Would I want to spend my precious Saturday afternoon watching the Blues? Has the club, in its present state, reached its plateau? I hope not, because there was certainly plenty of room for optimism – and bear in mind, they were plying their trade in Division One not that long ago. The facilities looked good and the stadium could be further developed; there are no rivals close by and the location is fantastic. Imagine if there was a bit more on offer in and around the stadium before the games, school football matches timed to finish before the senior team started and other sports and leisure facilities available within the stadium complex for multi-usage. Local amenities could be advertised for fans visiting with their families so that those who are so disposed can shop, lunch etc. Has there been a collective effort, involving schools, businesses, local council and the football club?

I thought about what it would be like to live in Stranraer and visit Stair Park regularly. A couple of beers in town (The Fitba' Bar sounds good), a short walk to the ground, a match in very pleasant surroundings, back into town for a few and then off home – a good day. With additional attractions at the football club it could be even more appealing; some lunch, a couple of beers with friends, leisure facilities for families. OK, my visit was during the summer, and winter in Stranraer can be horrendous (I've experienced it). Is there a case for covered stadiums? All in all, there's definite potential here. With some joined up thinking, this club should prosper.

Quote of the day – *Fan enquired about what hot food was available. Woman serving replied, 'Bacon rolls and Bovril!'*

GAME	STRANRAER VERSUS QUEEN'S PARK
DIVISION	SFL3
DATE	SAT 11 SEPT 2010, KO 3PM
VENUE	STAIR PARK, ATTENDANCE 408
SCORE	1-0

MATCH STATS:
HTTP://WWW.SCOTTISHFOOTBALLLEAGUE.COM/FOOTBALL/THIRD/RESULTS/3286142/

6

THE RED DEVILS V THE GERS

The Battle of Britain

FROM STAIR PARK to Old Trafford, Manchester, Scottish Division Three to the Champions League for the Battle of Britain – could the contrast be any greater? Manchester United v Rangers was not on the journey plan, but how could I resist an opportunity to sample some hospitality at one of the most famous football grounds in the world? The once-in-a-lifetime chance to see my very own club perform against the English legends was not to be missed. Several appointments were rescheduled and the obligatory phone call to the wife was made. All parties agreed and Manchester was a reality; well, almost.

The rest of the day was a mixture of excitement and worry, particularly regarding accommodation – would I get digs near the stadium at this late stage? Luckily, I managed to book into a hotel in Stockport which was actually much nearer than I thought. As I was checking in after a drive of just over three hours, I enquired about onward transport to Old Trafford. I thought about the other journeys I would take over the season. In terms of distance, few would be longer. However, the treks up to the Highlands and Peterhead would definitely be longer time-wise. Some serious planning would be required.

Taxi booked, I headed off to my room to get suited and booted. There was time to grab a pint whilst waiting on the taxi. Carling was my choice and I supped away, enjoying the drink, the free wi-fi and the surroundings – my hotel was a nice old converted rectory. A couple of phone calls were made to confirm arrangements and then I headed out to the waiting taxi. Twenty minutes later I was at my colleague's hotel. I texted him to let him know I was in the bar and ordered a drink, but was refused because I was a non-resident – apparently the police advice to licensed premises was not to sell alcohol to Rangers fans. I was eventually allowed to purchase the beer after I explained that

A proud Scotsman in Manchester

I wasn't about to go on the rampage and set the hotel on fire.

Next stop South Stand, Old Trafford. After a short taxi ride we were standing beneath the huge image of Sir Matt, the neon-lit Manchester United sign beaming into the dusk. The atmosphere went up a notch or two when the convoy of Rangers buses, all under police escort, started coming through. We were at a big game and there's no feeling quite like it. And, it's all because of the fans. You can talk all you like about competition, formats, TV coverage and money, goal-line technology… the single most important thing is the supporters of football clubs, and the sooner this is recognised and acted upon, the sooner the game will start to improve in Scotland.

We strolled towards the Munich Tunnel, only to be halted in our tracks by the police cordon that had formed to let the thousands of Gers fans pass through to the turnstiles. There were no problems whatsoever, but you could sense the police were a bit edgy, which was unfortunate. We enquired about passing through the cordon so as to reach our desired entry point. Permission granted, we carried on through to the plush doorway, flashed our leather-bound ticket holders and climbed the stairs to our lounge for the evening. This was

European football and trappings of the highest order – fabulous.

No need to worry about queuing for a half-time pie here, it would be served with the drinks of our choice during the break. The question was, would I need it after a four course meal? Food and drink were served promptly, although I was still munching on my main course when the teams lined up for that wonderful 'Zadok the Priest' anthem. The remaining items on my plate were devoured, drinks knocked back (no alcohol is allowed during games) and the seat was pushed in tight against the table so as to allow me stand and watch the action – much to the bewilderment of many of the regulars in the suite. One of my main disappointments was the fact we were actually inside the glass. I'd much rather be out in the open savouring the atmosphere to the full. Even so, the game was entertaining and overall Rangers put on a good show for Scotland. There was loads of criticism about their defensive formation but I honestly don't think they had any other option as the gulf in quality between the two leagues is significant.

The whistle blew for half time and we headed off for refreshments. I enjoyed a small steak pie and a pint and wondered why on earth I couldn't do this at Scottish grounds (outwith the hospitality suites). I have been at the Emirates Stadium where a similar policy is in operation. Surely it's time for a rethink north of the border.

The second half was under way as we emerged from behind the curtain that separates the area where alcohol can be served and the main arena. At Old Trafford there are many – perhaps too many – distractions for the regulars: mobiles, big TV screens and the fact that the seats don't actually face the park. The game itself wasn't generating much atmosphere, Rangers fans apart, and the place started emptying long before the final whistle. I now fully understood the comments made by former Manchester United Captain Roy Keane about the prawn sandwich brigade and their lack of enthusiasm for the team's efforts on the park. The folk here were totally different to the hospitality clientele I had encountered at Celtic Park, Ibrox and Hampden, where there is still fervent support in the executive boxes – another plus for Scottish football.

Game over, a well-deserved point on the board for the Glasgow team and, at last, some respect for the Scottish game restored. We ordered more drinks, took some photographs down in the South Stand and generally bantered about the game. There were a few Rangers fans in the suite and their presence became more apparent as the night wore on and drink loosened tongues – it was good-natured though. All too

Old Trafford – 100 years in the making.

Old Trafford – doesn't look it!

quickly the night drew to a close and we headed outside for a taxi. Forty minutes later and £38 lighter (the return journey was £18 more expensive than the outward one), I was back at the hotel and ready for bed. What a day, and night, it had been; watching Rangers at Old Trafford, watching Fergie walk the walk to his famous perch, watching Manchester United under the leadership of arguably Scotland's greatest manager – all in all, fantastic.

And the next game – TBC.

I travelled home the next day, jaded from one pint too many, but happy. The Champions League is where it's at, it's the holy grail, every player dreams of playing on that stage. I thought back to 1992 when it all started. Rangers were the British representatives, after defeating English champions Leeds United home and away (yes, the same Leeds United who played recently in the third tier of English football). Rangers narrowly missed out on a final spot. Marseille, who won the Gers' group, went on to win the final and were later charged by UEFA for irregularities. They were disappointed to come so close but much success followed, the pinnacle being the famous nine-in-a-row. How times have changed for Rangers, Leeds and Marseille.

For Manchester United, their recent success story was just beginning: season 1992/93 saw them lift their first top tier English title since 1968. In between, clubs including Aston Villa, Derby County and Nottingham Forest had all won the top trophy. Today it is almost inconceivable that any of these clubs could win it again – how times have changed.

Quote of the day – *Inebriated Rangers fan: 'We gubbed them nil nil!'*

GAME	MANCHESTER UNITED VERSUS RANGERS
DIVISION	CL
DATE	TUES 14 SEPT 2010, KO 7.45PM
VENUE	OLD TRAFFORD, ATTENDANCE 74,408
SCORE	0-0

MATCH STATS:
HTTP://WWW.MANUTD.COM/EN/FIXTURES-AND-RESULTS/MATCH
REPORTS/2010/SEP/UNITED-0-RANGERS-0.ASPX

7

THE BLUE BRAZIL V THE DEE

Taking Stock in Cowden

FROM THE RED DEVILS to the Blue Brazil, another amazing contrast and one that is unlikely to happen again on the journey. So, Fife it was, though the garden is absolutely screaming at me, the pups too. I was getting a wee bit annoyed about missing all the sunshine – I should have been down the beach on a day like this. Anyway, time to go. The SatNav displayed an arrival time of 2.37, which was probably a bit neat considering I had no idea where to park. An hour and a half later I was crawling up the bustling main street worrying that I might miss kick off.

Panic over, I hurried past some artificial pitches and into the entrance of what looked like a car breaker's yard. I was amazed at the state of the place. I asked a steward where the home support enter. 'Chapel Street,' was his reply, 'if you don't have a season ticket.' This just happened to be at the other end of the ground. After a brisk walk the turnstile was in my sights. I approached cautiously because I had set a precedent at previous games of a stand seat, and wanted to maintain some consistency. I enquired about stand seating and the attendant confirmed this was the way in, charged me an incredible £17 and stuffed my new £20 note into his wad of cash – welcome to Central Park.

My route to the stand took me across the open and empty terracing at the west end of this huge ground. The expanse was sporadically populated by groups of men, some with dogs, and the odd teenager wandering aimlessly up and down the concrete. I felt uneasy as I walked through, obviously a stranger in these parts, unaware of the customs and practices at Cowden games. I did my usual scan of the surroundings looking for toilets and snack bars. The only toilets were Portaloos, four in total, and the snack bar was a caravan adjacent to the stand. I was dreading my half-time pie and Bovril already. I bought a programme, chose a second row seat (bad choice), and tried to settle down for my first experience of the Blue Brazil. However, my seat was uncomfortable, the view was terrible and the pitch was miles away – why do people put up with these conditions, week in week out? There is a distinct lack of respect for the supporters – expecting them to turn up every other week at this dump is outrageous.

The stadium seemed strangely familiar. I knew I had never been to a football match here but something was niggling away. I thought of the speedway at Shawfield – there were some similarities. A couple of days later it came to me – stock car racing – and I immediately texted my dad, who was holidaying in Spain. 'Have you ever taken me to stock car racing in Cowdenbeath?' was the question. 'Yes,' was the instant reply. I had indeed experienced Central Park, which had probably changed little since my last visit *circa* 1975.

I flicked through the programme (for some reason it reminded me of a *Broons* book) trying to evaluate the content but I couldn't concentrate properly as I was still getting over my shock at the state of my surroundings. The place was falling apart. Whatever licence it needs to operate is surely in danger of being revoked – this stadium actually made Somerset Park look salubrious.

The teams ran out. In theory, this should be a good contest between a team expected to be fighting for promotion and one that was punching above its weight; all the ingredients for a cracking game of football on what was my reintroduction to the First Division. During the seconds before kick off, I wondered how Jimmy Nicholl, the Cowdenbeath manager, handled the stadium tour with any potential signings. How do you sell this place to a footballer? 'Come and ply your trade in the middle of a race-track, surrounded by old tyres, crash barriers and "Motor Sport is Dangerous" signs.' All credit to Jimmy for believing in the Blue Brazil.

Game on, and my first impressions were that Dundee looked the more professional outfit, smarter, slicker and fitter than their hosts. Cowden were undoubtedly hungrier though, and their positive, attacking football resulted in a two-goal lead for most of the match. There seemed to be a lot of misplaced passes and overly high balls and I wondered if this was in some way down to the surroundings. The stadium was a huge open space with only one side built up to any extent, the rest being sloping terraces. Would passing be more precise in a stadium where the crowd were close to the touchlines, the four

Is this a football match?

sides hemmed in the pitch and physically the link between fans and players was closer?

Although it was entertaining throughout, the match was probably the worst, in technical terms, of the seven games I'd seen so far in the season. Credit must go to the home support, who got behind their team from start to finish. The same couldn't be said of the Dundee fans, who were only woken from their slumber when their heroes scored with minutes to go. Lots of them left early and I was a bit disappointed by their performance.

The final whistle signalled the end of the game and the home fans were absolutely delighted. Much shouting (it's amazing how brave some people are from the back of stands), singing and celebrating. The Dundee management team were constantly goaded about picking up their P45s, which was imminent, according to the Cowden faithful. During the game I had thought a lot about the type of people surrounding me and I couldn't help but put them in the unemployed category – that's maybe why they were so fervent in their baiting of the Dundee coaches. After what seemed like an absolute age, I eventually managed to get out of the breaker's yard and set off for home.

What a day it had been, a real experience. My mind was racing as I struggled through the traffic and headed south towards the Forth Road Bridge. The journey home, on a different route, was also different in terms of all the football pitches that were now empty. The drive earlier this afternoon had highlighted how much football goes on in Scotland. Not only were many of the pitches in use, the roads were also packed full of cars and coaches heading to games – this is a huge industry.

Time for a rant. Football is fundamental to Scottish culture and, arguably more importantly, the economy. Talk of the leagues in this country as being 'Mickey Mouse' is completely off the mark. It should be recognised that they are essential to the wellbeing of many of the people. Standards need to improve but let's not forget we have thousands of very loyal followers of the product that is Scottish football.

Rant over, back to the Blue Brazil. I have probably been over-critical of the club, based on my initial observations of the goings-on in and around the stadium. However, there is definitely potential; if supporters regularly come to this place in numbers, they would go anywhere. On further perusal, the programme turned out to be quite interesting; not your usual shiny production, which seems to be the norm, but more personal and with some good reading. Two sections particularly caught my attention.

Firstly, a look back at Cowdenbeath in the pre Premier League years when 20 teams, with names like Clyde, Queens Park and Bo'ness in among them, made up the First Division. (I wondered about the appeal of such a big league. The very reason we changed to a ten-team set-up was to try and raise standards. This has not happened and we need to expand the leagues again). Secondly, there was an interesting piece on Scottish juvenile football, which was described as the third tier behind the seniors and juniors, which ended 20 years ago. Do we focus too much on the tip of the iceberg? Over the past few years the answer is probably yes, but that is changing and many clubs, Cowdenbeath included, now have academies in place to develop the footballers of tomorrow.

Stand seating – is that what you call it?

And the future for the 'Beath: worrying, yes, but this club's not a lost cause. I know I have banged on about multi-usage for stadiums; however, in this case I don't think it works well. The facilities adjacent to the stadium (leisure centre and artificial pitches etc) looked reasonably good and there was space on the perimeter that could be developed. The locals love their club without a doubt, the Cowdenbeath fans are as passionate as I've come across, and this can only bode well for the future. The stadium is a major problem though, and lots of thought from lots of people is required. Personally, I like towns the size of Cowdenbeath, there's enough to keep you amused and interested, and if I stayed there I would go to all the games at Central Park. However, with a population of approximately 12,000, how many can we really expect at games on a regular basis, bearing in mind the close proximity of other football clubs.

The whole package has to be more appealing to draw people in, and this is something that has to be addressed, not only by the Blue Brazil but by Scottish football in general.

Quote of the day – Cowden fan: 'It's like watching Brazil.' Aye, right, I thought to myself.

GAME	COWDENBEATH VERSUS DUNDEE
DIVISION	SFL1
DATE	SAT 25 SEPT 2010, KO 3PM
VENUE	CENTRAL PARK, ATTENDANCE 1,154
SCORE	2-1

MATCH STATS:
HTTP://WWW.SCOTTISHFOOTBALLLEAGUE.COM/FOOTBALL/FIRST/
RESULTS/3286274/

8

THE DOONHAMERS V THE PARS

Hammering the Pars

WITH GAME 8 IMMINENT, my options ranged between Berwick in the borders, Raith Rovers in Fife or Queen of the South in Dumfries. After discussions with the wife, I settled on Dumfries as she wanted to have a day out in Berwick (but not today) and to visit friends in Fife (but hadn't contacted them). So, into the mobile comfort zone and off down the A76. I really don't know how governments around the world are going to get people out of their cars. In fact they're not, so stop messing about, develop clean green cars and build better, safer roads. I don't mind public transport, but unfortunately for the environment it's just so much easier by car.

It was raining, so I felt much better about going to a match and had no guilty thoughts about the garden or longings to spend time on the beach. Summer football – the jury's still out on that one as far as I'm concerned.

I enjoyed my drive south, football on the radio (Hearts v Rangers, injury-time winner for the Gers), very little traffic and a reasonably good average speed, which took a few minutes off the journey time. On the road through deepest, darkest Ayrshire, I probably saw more signs for football pitches than I did people. With towns so deserted I wondered how the junior leagues could be so vibrant.

Dumfries was getting closer and there still wasn't a lot in terms of football traffic. The first scarves dangling from windows were spotted at the strange rectangular 'roundabout' with the big footbridge, heading in a different direction from me – you must trust the SatNav though. Eventually, via the town centre, I was outside the ground. The Palmerston Park floodlights looked dated and somewhat menacing against the battleship grey backdrop. This is 'real' football, I thought to myself; travelling to different places, unfamiliar surroundings, a far cry from standing in a pub or sitting at home, although there is definitely a place for that too – still need to get to the fitba' though.

The week's news had been dominated by the 'Will he? Won't he?' saga regarding Barry Ferguson and Scotland. 'He won't' was the outcome – I was surprised. As a Hampden regular for international matches, I would walk over broken glass with numerous bits of my anatomy on fire to pull on that jersey. Could it be that there was more to the Ferguson scenario than met the eye?

I followed the trickle of Doonhamers faithful down through an empty supermarket car park towards the Main Stand. It was strange that it was located so close to the stadium. Usually nowadays the pattern is that the supermarket chain buys the football ground, builds a new stadium for the club and everyone lives happily ever after. Maybe the club had sold some land and this now abandoned supermarket was the outcome. If so, the club have certainly limited their opportunities for redevelopment of the stadium, which is surrounded by houses and other buildings. Stadiums that have complementary facilities close by definitely have a broader appeal. They seem more useful, more modern and generally more sporty than those that are restricted by their location.

The entrance to the Main Stand was a pleasing hive of activity. I purchased the programme and entered through the smallest turnstile ever built, I couldn't even see the guy (why is that the case sometimes?), and headed up the stairs. The main concourse was busy and I was tempted to go for a pint in the lounge bar, which looked very welcoming with the doors wide open. I had second thoughts when I realised that

Lounging around

everyone was seated and that this was probably the hospitality section.

I headed for the back row of plastic seats, as usual taking a seat towards the end of a row. My chosen pew, which wasn't marked 'reserved', was unfortunately the usual spot for an elderly couple who bestowed derogatory looks on me until I enquired if all was OK. The reply was congenial enough and I asked if they wanted me to move – 'No no,' was the reply. Content that I was not upsetting local customs I settled down with my shiny programme.

I was surrounded by significantly more older people than I had experienced at the games so far this season, and the noise levels were definitely a few decibels lower. The game threatened to be a cracker and I had been expecting a better atmosphere so I was bit disappointed. Although thinking back to last week and the Blue Brazil, this was definitely a step up in class.

The last time I had seen Queens was at Hampden in the 2008 Scottish Cup Final when they were narrowly beaten by Rangers. I anticipated that today's game against the high flying Pars would be another close encounter and, sure enough, the two teams were up and at each other from the off. The same couldn't be said for the fans, particularly the home lot, but the subdued atmosphere didn't impact on any of the players, who sustained a high tempo throughout, even when the rain was lashing down. I really enjoyed the game. The lower division sides definitely have more of a go at winning rather than, for example, settling for a point, and this is refreshing.

The half-time whistle caught me busily checking the scores on the iPhone. Somewhat startled, I headed for the snack bar where the queue was lining up directly in front of the toilets and the table with all the condiments on it – is somebody missing something here? Anyway, the service was prompt and it was nice to see three generations serving behind the counter. The food was reasonably good, chips and a Bovril this time (I'm sick of pies), and the place looked very clean – so much better than those caravans that I had been subjected to over the past couple of weeks.

The floodlights were on for the second half – the first time this season for a daytime game – and the match started to get really interesting which was mostly down to the diabolical performance from the away goalie. Two quick goals for the Doonhamers, one a howler from the keeper and the other an audacious lob (keeper at fault again), and the game was over as a contest even with the late sending off for the home side. All in all, there was plenty good football on show, particularly

Grandstand, is that what you call it?

from Allan 'Magic' Johnston. I had expected to see many more old pros in the lower division games, however this tradition seems to be petering out – a pity, because some of the players coming through are definitely too young, both mentally and physically, which could be dangerous in a number of ways.

Game over, and I started to gather my thoughts on the Dumfriesshire club. I had been to McDiarmid Park and Hampden already that week for meetings and Palmerston Park wasn't in the same league in terms of facilities. Nevertheless, there was obvious potential. For a town with a population of around 35,000 and limited competition close by, the support could be better.

The stadium was OK, I liked the terraced sections at each end and it would have been great to see them full. The wooden main stand got me thinking about the fire at Bradford City. Hopefully the housekeeping regime here is well monitored. There were plenty of exit signs but why don't they hang them a bit higher – some obstruct the view.

The drive home was pleasurable, usually is when you get a double up. I had enjoyed my afternoon and was pleased that the club had potential. The Doonhamers are without doubt better placed than many of their rivals in the division. The programme showcased the successful Junior Blues youth programme and the Queen's Trust, both interesting ventures. As at Clyde and Motherwell, the trust aims to involve the community in all aspects of football, from local to international. This integration is key to the future of football and for a healthier society in general. With proper management, which must be about systemic inclusion of all stakeholders in the local area, the club should have a bright future.

Next up, The Czech Republic and then the World champions, Spain. Does it get any better than this – Scottish football in decline?

Quote of the day – *Doonhamer's fan: 'Have we signed their goalie?'*

GAME	QUEEN OF THE SOUTH VERSUS DUNFERMLINE
DIVISION	SFL1
DATE	SAT 2 OCT 2010, KO 3PM
VENUE	PALMERSTON PARK, ATTENDANCE 2,139
SCORE	2-0

MATCH STATS:
HTTP://WWW.SCOTTISHFOOTBALLLEAGUE.COM/FOOTBALL/FIRST/
RESULTS/3283084/

9

SCOTLAND V SPAIN

The Beautiful Game

NO CHOICES FOR this week's game... well almost, I could have headed for Elgin or Montrose on Saturday but decided to have the weekend off and focus my attention on the midweek international.

Where do I start? After an excruciatingly bad night in Prague, we now faced the World and European Champions at Hampden. The Spanish were in town and the odds were stacked against us. The last thing we needed was another doing, but it looked like it was on the cards.Hampden, here I come.

After attending a training course at Clydebank College, I headed straight for the national stadium. The traffic was very busy, a major problem with midweek games, and it was after six before I was parked and on my way up towards Battlefield in search of the lads and a pint. Church on the Hill was as busy as I've ever seen it, it was absolutely stowed out, and I quickly phoned the lads who were on the way from the city centre to tell them the bad news. We changed venue to The Ivory and I rushed down the hill only to find another mobbed boozer. It's murder trying to get a pint around here. I persevered and after about 15 minutes had one in each hand. The lads duly arrived and immediately had second thoughts on attempting to get served. The decision was to get a carry-out and take their chances on the street – it's unbelievable how hard it is to get a pint with your mates near the ground before a big international game... something's not right. I finished my drinks and left for the ground via a wee off-sales where I purchased a can that was swiftly downed in the shadows of the tenements on Sinclair Drive – all very sad.

Forty-five minutes to kick off, I was going through the turnstiles at the 'Rangers end' and up into the main arena for the first time since my visit to see Queen's Park. the place was relatively empty and I

Fireworks at Hampden

purchased my evening meal (steak pie, chips and Bovril – £5.50), no queue whatsoever. That got me thinking. Why on earth could I not meet my mates in here and have a few beers alongside something to eat? There's plenty of room, it's well supervised and it certainly beats any of those overcrowded pubs where everyone is throwing drink down their necks as fast as they can. This is a no-brainer. Will someone please wake up and smell the coffee – or the lager, for that matter. Alcohol is available in all the hospitality suites, so why not let the rest of us fans have a wee drink before the game, close the bars during it and reopen after the final whistle. In other words, encourage sensible, controlled drinking without the rushing and binging that currently afflicts our supporters and our national reputation as a whole. If only!

Apologies, ranting again, but it's definitely time for a review.

Back to the football, and the atmosphere was building nicely. The old Hampden roar is special and it reached a crescendo just before kick off. A pity it's is already the most dated 'modern' stadium in the world.

One thing was certain, the fans would back the team even after last Friday's debacle against the Czech Republic. I still can't believe that we played without a striker. Blatantly an opportunity lost, and by the end of the night I was bitterly disappointed and confused.

Back to tonight's action. Firecrackers exploded, national anthems sung, and we're off. This was £25 well spent. The Spaniards were a joy to watch, definitely the best team I could remember seeing in the flesh. Scotland didn't look too bad either and they were a touch unlucky to be one down at the break. The world champions upped the ante after the half-time singsong (not the best I've ever experienced) and quickly doubled their lead. They oozed confidence and I'm sure this self-belief is down to their ball control. Every one of them was so comfortable in possession, they moved the ball swiftly yet never seemed to be in a rush – the beautiful game, played beautifully. But hold on, this is Scotland at Hampden, we don't care how good you are, we'll still get stuck in. Two quick goals, one of which was very good, and all of a sudden the Spaniards were rattled. Could the unthinkable happen, could we come from two down and snatch a winner against the best team in the world? For a wee while they looked shell-shocked and it was a lovely possibility, but they regrouped, Scotland seemed to take their foot off the gas a touch and the inevitable third goal came for the opposition.

In hindsight, Spain could probably have gone up another few gears if required. Even in defeat, this was a much better performance from Scotland than the previous one, and more importantly, a game that was entertaining. But where do we go from here?

'We Stand Together' was the header on the official programme, and I've no doubt we will. However, qualification for the next Euros looks unlikely and with the under-21s failing at the final play-off stage, major tournaments are becoming a thing of the past for Scotland. There is a monkey on our back that we need to get rid of, and quickly – and the only way this can happen is if all the stakeholders in the game recognise that the international team is the pinnacle of Scottish football. Too many of our clubs have their own agendas and while to an extent this is understandable, it often means they are pulling in different directions. There is nothing that gets the country going more than the prospect of a big international match, especially if we have a chance of getting a result. So why doesn't the international team take precedence over everything else football-wise? This is where the leadership aspect has to come to the fore. If we had one organisation controlling the game in Scotland, rather than three, then we might start to make an impact on the stages that really matter.

There are currently too many cooks. The SFA, SFL and SPL all have their own mandates, aims and objectives. They have to look after their respective stakeholders, so it's inevitable that there will be conflict – with the loser being the game of football itself.

How many more international tournaments will I get the chance to go to? Euro 2012 is another showpiece that the Tartan Army will miss. Brazil 2014 is the next target and fingers crossed we get there, failing that its back to the drawing board for France 2016, 18 years on since we last qualified for a major tournament – scary.

Everyone needs to be pulling in the same direction and a single organisation with representatives from across the football spectrum is what we need to deliver this.

Quote of the day – Scotland fans (on numerous occasions): 'Come on get into this lot they're pish.' They're the world champions.

GAME	SCOTLAND VERSUS SPAIN
DIVISION	EURO 2012 QUALIFIER
DATE	TUES 12 OCT 2010, KO 8PM
VENUE	HAMPDEN PARK, ATTENDANCE, 51,322
SCORE	2-3

MATCH STATS:
HTTP://WWW.SCOTTISHFA.CO.UK/INTERNATIONAL_FIXTURE_DETAILS.CFM?PAGE=2853&MATCHID=96710

10

LIVI LIONS V THE WARRIORS

No Fight from the Warriors

ANNAN, ARBROATH AND MONTROSE from Division Three, and Peterhead from Division Two, were all possibilities. The wife was having a wee moan about my escapades and I decided to have another look. Livingston quickly became an option and I could also offer the 'other half' a day out at a big shopping centre. This was duly proposed, and after much deliberation, rejected ('Don't know the shops, too much to carry') – you can but try.

Anyway, I had done some research on the club and decided to go for it. Timewise it was the preferable option and I knew it wouldn't take up the whole day – Almondvale Stadium here I come.

En route I fumed about another missed opportunity in the garden – and probably be my last chance before bad weather became the norm. The run over to East Kilbride and along the M8 was strangely quiet. There was virtually no football traffic. I knew roughly where the stadium was, however the old SatNav was in charge and issuing instructions that I followed to the letter. The route was different from the one I had in mind and I felt as if I was going round in circles – Livingston drives me mad. As usual, the navigation system got it right and suddenly I was in the queue for the car park right next to the stadium. The first steward directed me onwards to her colleague, who she described as 'the robber'. I was charged £5 for the pleasure of parking, which is probably a bit steep, but in hindsight it made things so much easier for my inaugural visit.

I strolled all the way round and was impressed by the sports, business and leisure facilities on offer in the modern stadium. Its easy accessibility from Edinburgh should have some benefits as well as the fact that there are no other big clubs locally. Its proximity to Livingston town centre was a definite plus – lots of people were walking to the

Not much 'roaring' back here

ground and by the time I got to the main entrance there were plenty of supporters in evidence. The atmosphere was building nicely.

While choosing a turnstile, I suddenly noticed that I wasn't actually at Almondvale Stadium: signs announced that I was about to enter the 'Braidwood Motors Stadium'. Had the trusty SatNav taken me to the wrong place? But no, Braidwood Motors Stadium it was.

Changing the names of stadiums to reflect sponsorship is something that often gets the fans up in arms. Personally, I see no problem with it – in fact, good on everyone concerned at Livi for generating both advertising and much needed revenue from the stadium name. It was also good to see references to Meadowbank Thistle (and Ferranti), both at the ground and on the website (hopefully, the remaining senior clubs in Scotland can avoid their fate).

Resisting the temptations of the Stadium Bar, I went through the turnstile, parted with £12 and walked out into the main arena at pitch level. I was impressed with the overall set-up so far – a newish stadium, good sports facilities surrounding the ground and plenty of lounges for hospitality on match days that, more importantly, can be used for other events.

Game on, and it's back to the 'real football' after the trials and tribulations of losing to Spain at Hampden during the week. One would naturally expect a lower standard here and there was indeed a big difference, although the style of football from Livingston was not short on quality. Quick, crisp passing was the norm, with some excellent play. Stenhousemuir were stunned by the tempo of the game and quickly went 3-0. On the verge of a hammering, they made a stab at a recovery, grabbing a goal to bring it back to 3-1. But their fight-back was short-lived as the Lions regained their three-goal advantage.

The last time I'd seen a Livingston team live had been back at Ibrox in the SPL when Ronald de Boer and company were resident in Glasgow. I think the game finished 4-3 to Rangers but it was a cracker, really entertaining – how things have changed for both clubs.

I found I'd regained my appetite for steak pie (which was very good) and enjoyed a Bovril (I'll never lose my appetite for Bovril!) before settling down for the second half, which was dull compared to the first.

It was without doubt getting colder. Sitting for long periods outside can be a chilly business and I wondered if it would be warmer standing on a covered terrace. The lack of atmosphere was also having a dampening effect on my enthusiasm, there was virtually no singing whatsoever from the home fans and the away support was non-existent. The managers made a few changes but the game had been over as a contest by half time.

I exited the car park with minimum fuss. Again the roundabouts confused me but thankfully the SatNav got me to the M8 and it was retired to the glove box. Today's football, from a Livingston perspective, had been very good.

Stenny were not in the same league and I imagined their season would be a struggle. They had some of the smallest, skinniest players I can remember seeing, which got me thinking of the Scotland v France match a few years ago. The French were taller and looked more powerful than the Scots, but we beat them, home and away. However, there are many very young players in Scotland's lower leagues and I'm concerned that some of these guys are just not ready to play football at these levels.

I came away impressed by both Livingston's infrastructure and the football, and wondering why the attendance was so low – the stadium was almost empty. Of around 50,000 people living in one of the most populated areas in the Lothians, surely more could be enticed along than the 2,000 people who spent their afternoon here. Perhaps it's down to the club's turbulent history.

In their early years, the Lions roared up through the divisions and the fans flocked to see them. But then they went into administration, lost Premier League status, and as League Cup winners in season

2003/04, dropped back to the Third Division – a complete turnaround. Still, everything is in place and the football the team are playing is good, and certainly merits more fans clicking through the turnstiles.

Quote of the day – *Car park steward: 'Pay the robber over there.' (Referring to the attendant collecting the £5 parking fee.)*

GAME	LIVINGSTON VERSUS STENHOUSEMUIR
DIVISION	SFL2
DATE	SAT 16 OCT 2010, KO 3PM
VENUE	ALMONDVALE STADIUM, ATTENDANCE 1,606
SCORE	4-1

MATCH STATS:
HTTP://WWW.SCOTTISHFOOTBALLLEAGUE.COM/FOOTBALL/SECOND/
RESULTS/3283181/

11

THE BINOS V THE JAGS

Sterling in Stirling

I WAS STRUGGLING to motivate myself for a game after a very late return home from down south the night before – it's hard graft being a football fan. Today's main choices, SPL apart, ranged from East Fife, to Stenhousemuir, to Stirling. The First Division side got the vote. Partick Thistle were the visitors and I was looking forward to a good game. My usual Saturday chores done and dusted, and traffic info checked, by 1.15 I was on the road north. I had a good run until roadworks on the A80 slowed things down and I got a bit anxious as we hit some traffic on the numerous roundabouts on the A91. A missed exit added to my unease, as I would now have to travel on to the next roundabout, which seemed like miles away, and about turn.

Eventually I got there. My research had indicated that there was ample parking adjacent to Forthbank Stadium but the car park was full, much to my annoyance, and the burly attendant was waving all the traffic up the road where, thankfully, there were plenty of parking places.

First impressions were favourable. Swimming pools, health clubs and floodlit, all-weather pitches surround the stadium, making for a vibrant sporting environment. This type of set-up is definitely my preference, with the football club at the centre of a variety of sports activities and facilities – the jewel in the crown, the focus for all the budding sportspeople... oh, dreaming again. Time to part with some hard-earned cash.

Programme purchased (£2), I passed through the turnstile to the right of the stadium reception, handed over £16 for the pleasure, and found myself right beside the snack bar queue. As usual I wasn't impressed with the catering set-up and decided to purchase my lunch right away and avoid the half-time scrum. The line moved reasonably

Club shop's quiet!

quickly (probably because I was enjoying the music that was blasting out over the PA) and suddenly I was being questioned by the server as to my requirements – there was no menu on the wall. I instinctively asked for a steak pie and Bovril, which were duly produced – who needs a menu when you go to football in Scotland. The servers were very nice and so was the food. Now for the game.

I opted for a seat near the front of the stand, hoping I hadn't taken someone's usual pew. There were lots of seats with reserved icons on them and it was at this point that I remembered that the fans owned the club – though I'm not sure of the intricacies of the arrangement. So, not only might I be sitting on a season ticket holder's seat, he or she might actually own part of the club as well. I checked under the seat: no plastic tag. I was OK, so I proceeded to finish my late lunch, enjoying the stunning views over to the Trossachs. The setting even beat Stranraer. The modern, functional stadium had two stands and two terraced ends. Ideal, I thought. Unfortunately, the terraces were empty. The away support were directly opposite me and I was impressed by the turnout. Many had obviously made the journey from Glasgow, without doubt Scotland's football capital.

Within two minutes the Binos took the lead with the fastest goal I'd seen this season and suddenly the almost silent mix of Albion regulars

What a backdrop!

started to make some noise. The home side were dominating the early stages when they were surprisingly pegged back by an equaliser from Thistle. This didn't deter them though, and they scored another two before half time. There were more high balls than usual, but generally the game was entertaining and the pitch looked good as well. The Glaswegians were easily drowning out the home support and this was a disappointing aspect. I wondered how many students had taken up the offer of free entry, they certainly weren't obvious in the crowd although there was a bit of a rammy in the away stand – perhaps some had sneaked in there to wind up the opposing support. Just before half time, an elderly gentleman returned from the snack bar complaining that they had run out of steak pies – just as well I'd purchased mine upon entry, as I don't think I'll ever eat another Scotch pie again after that Fir Park offering.

Half time and 3-1 to the Albion. The sun was going down and I was starting to feel the cold. I dread to think what the place must be like on a wet and windy winter's day. During the break I studied the programme. It was very encouraging to see all the youth development that's going on and of course the fans buying into the club. It was apparent here that there is a fervent and loyal support. Do fans like these receive in turn an equivalent level of commitment from the authorities and other leaders within the Scottish game?

Back to the fitba', and it's all go; strange decisions, late tackles and everything else that makes the game in this country so special (and we've got the Old Firm game to look forward to as well tomorrow). Another couple of second-half goals, some sublime touches from the veteran Jackie McNamara (it's always good to see a top player moving back down the leagues). Overall, it was an entertaining and enjoyable experience at Forthbank Stadium. I just wish more than 1,386 fans had been there to see it.

Listening to the results coming in on the drive home was especially enjoyable when I got a wee treble up.

Back to the Binos. The population of Stirling is approximately 40,000, so why so few fans today? I reckon that the away support made up about 500, leaving only 900 home supporters. There are numerous senior clubs in the surrounding area, possibly too many, and this may be an issue. The infrastructure is in place and the fans own 100 per cent of the club, the first senior club with this status according to its website. The fans having a direct say in the running of the club is a great idea. Hopefully it will work out well in the long term – I sincerely hope that this is not as good as it gets for Stirling Albion.

Quote of the day – *Stirling fan: 'We could still make the Premier, you know.'*

GAME	STIRLING ALBION VERSUS PARTICK THISTLE
DIVISION	SFL1
DATE	SAT 23 OCT 2010, KO 3PM
VENUE	FORTHBANK STADIUM, ATTENDANCE 1,386
SCORE	4-2

MATCH STATS.
HTTP://WWW.SCOTTISHFOOTBALLLEAGUE.COM/FOOTBALL/FIRST/
RESULTS/3283256/

12

THE JAM TARTS V KILLIE

Killie-ing the Atmosphere

COULDN'T BE BOTHERED going to a game on Saturday for a number of reasons – a hangover being the primary one. I had earmarked Annan but whilst studying my coupon I noticed this one wasn't on it. I checked the website which confirmed it had been postponed, so back to the drawing board. My plan had been to avoid SPL and First Division matches during the better weather as they are more likely to go ahead in the winter with the undersoil heating and the other paraphernalia that the bigger clubs have at their disposal. However, my protocol went right out of the window when I noticed Hearts were hosting my local SPL team, Kilmarnock. Edinburgh, here I come. A 12.45 kick off in the capital on the sleepy Sunday after the clocks went back. I hadn't been too keen on this start time when I took in the game at Fir Park, so we'd see how we got on today.

I was still on the M77 in Glasgow when the queuing began to agitate me. The roadworks could seriously disrupt my planning. It would be difficult to park at Tynecastle and I'd wanted to leave plenty of time for finding a space, photographs and general familiarisation. Thankfully, after the hold-up I got a clear run through until the SatNav displayed half a mile to the ground, and all of a sudden the place was mobbed.

I decided to try my luck on various side streets close to the ground, but to no avail. Getting more and more annoyed, I headed further from the stadium with the clock ticking down towards kick off. I found a space on Whitson Terrace (easily a mile away), and hurried back towards the protruding steelwork in the distance – all of a sudden the £5 I'd parted with at Livi a couple of weeks ago was the best I'd ever spent. This was a nightmare. In through Sainsbury's, under a couple of low railway bridges and then a left turn onto Wheatfield Place and the Wheatfield Stand loomed large. I was quite surprised at how big it

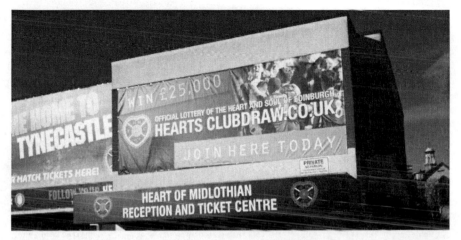

The heart and soul of Gorgie

was, TV pictures don't do it justice. Typically, I was at the wrong end and would have to circle the entire stadium to gain entry. I worked my way through the throng, all going in the opposite direction to me, and eventually reached the turnstiles at the Roseburn Stand where I handed over £22 and, with minutes to spare, climbed the stairs into Tynecastle for the first time.

Up to this point I had joined the home fans in the Main Stand areas to try and get a feel for the locals and the club. However, this could sometimes be difficult, especially in bigger clubs with season-ticket-holder and other restrictions. So I had decided on the away section and confirmed with the ticket office on the Saturday that there was indeed a pay gate. I was pleased to be issued with a ticket which, along with the programme (£3), I regard as important memorabilia. No time to read it yet. The noise levels were rising, whipped up by the announcer, and the game was about to burst into life. What a great pre-match atmosphere.

The two teams went at each other from the word go, playing fast and furious football on a sun-bathed pitch that looked immaculate. End-to-end stuff, Killie the better team. It looked like honours would be even when I decided to head down to the snack bar a couple of minutes before half time. And yes, right on the whistle Killie scored and the stand above me erupted. Unfortunately, there were no big screens on the concourse, just an old telly mounted high above the bookie's counter. Normally I waited until the break before heading for a snack, but having sized up the small outlet as I rushed up into the

Bastion Tynecastle

stand before kick off I knew I would have to be sharp to get served and return to my pew in time for the second half. This decision meant that I missed the goal on the stroke of half time.

Sadly, the catering service was to the usual Scottish football standard, with pies and hot drinks the main fare and a huge queue to grow the appetite. I stood and ate my steak pie and supped my Bovril, looking around at a huge space that could be put to vastly better use. For the fans, travelling ones in particular, clubs could do so much more in terms of basic hospitality. This only underlines what I said in my rant about Hampden: why can't people come here early, have a beer, coffee (decent type) or sandwich before the game, in comfortable, safe surroundings?

Back to the football. Hearts came roaring out of the traps for the second half. They created a few chances but it just wasn't their day and Killie picked them off, scoring another two superb goals in the process. The game was over as a contest well before the end and there was no need for the disappointing behaviour that marred the closing stages. The ridiculous play-acting, time-wasting and whingeing at officials is nowhere near as prevalent in the lower leagues. I don't subscribe to the argument that there's more pressure in the top division – it's simply down to culture. The pressure the guys are under in the lower leagues to keep their clubs alive is serious, yet they don't resort to the negative antics that we see week in, week out, in the SPL and other major leagues in Europe. And while I'm on the subject, the outcry against referees and linesmen often reaches fever pitch. It has to be recognised that this incessant criticism is damaging the game and that all stakeholders have a responsibility to act in the appropriate manner, whether managers, journalists or individuals posting on the web.

Yet another rant. That's what this religion that is Scottish football does to you, it's all-consuming.

Next on the agenda is kick-off time. After today's game I was back on the road mid-afternoon. An early kick off makes travel safer in the winter, allows more time for evening activities and could even reduce drunkenness at games. Possibly there should be a variety of kick-off times to suit the fans and the clubs, rather than setting them to suit the TV schedulers.

The size of the crowd at Tynecastle (13,056) was a bit of a disappointment, even though it felt much busier than that. I had expected a full house as Hearts had the chance to go third in the league. How many would have been in the ground if they could have gone top or had been challenging for the championship? The obvious question is, should Celtic and Rangers leave the SPL if they could? My response would be yes: without the perpetual dominance of the Old Firm, other clubs would benefit from the opportunity to win more trophies and compete in Europe. Whatever happens, the Jambos have tremendous potential but their 'Should we stay or go?' decision regarding the stadium is going to be a hard call.

A club's stadium should be more than just an arena for playing the beautiful game. The days of blowing away the cobwebs every other week are over. These places have got to earn their keep and this has been recognised by the club and the local community leaders. The opportunities for further developing Tynecastle are limited and the club feel this is hindering their future development. As the *Daily Record* reported, 'The stadium is no longer compliant with UEFA regulations, nor does it enable the club to attract the level of income they require from wider sources, such as conferences, events and corporate hospitality'. A formal decision has yet to been made but I suspect that a new stadium in a different location is the desired option and it would make sense. Now I know that generations of Hearts' fans consider Tynecastle their spiritual home and it will be hard to uproot and go elsewhere. But times change and so must the fans and clubs. A new community complex with purpose-built facilities will benefit the club in a variety of ways. The academy set-up at Heriot Watt University is a shining example of what can be achieved in partnership. This modern facility on the university campus will develop the players of the future and should be an important building block for Heart of Midlothian in the 21st century.

Much food for thought. But enough talk about football for at least a day (Monday) and then let's look forward to the Champions League on Tuesday. It would be good to see Hearts in it one day.

Quote of the day – *Drunk Kilmarnock fan in front of me: 'Whit's that smell? It's always the same here.' (It happens to be a brewery.)*

GAME	HEARTS VERSUS KILMARNOCK
DIVISION	SPL
DATE	SUN 31 OCT 2010, KO 12.45PM
VENUE	TYNECASTLE STADIUM, ATTENDANCE 13,056
SCORE	0-3

MATCH STATS:
HTTP://WWW.SCOTPREM.COM/CONTENT/DEFAULT.ASP?PAGE=S12_1_1
&WORKINGDATE=2010-10-31

13

THE BUDDIES V THE GERS

The Budding Buddies

AS I WAS ATTENDING a graduation ceremony on the Saturday, I had no option other than the sole fixture on the Sabbath – St Mirren Park, the Buddies playing the Gers. It was a sluggish start to the day after the excesses of the night before, but a good walk down the beach with the wife cleared the cobwebs and we had the brainwave to go out for Sunday breakfast – not something we do very often. Around 9.30, as we were strolling along the main street in Prestwick, I spotted a Northern Ireland Rangers supporters bus picking up some locals waiting at the cross. It struck me that they were going to be very early for the 12.45 kick off and so at the restaurant I checked the kick-off time on the iPhone, only to discover that it was a midday start.

There was absolutely no way I could sit amongst other supporters when my own team were out on the pitch, so it was the West Stand for me, in amongst the substantial travelling support. I had some difficulty getting the ticket. 'They're sold out,' the Saints ticket office attendant barked at me when I phoned, and when I enquired about the possibility of a 'St Mirren end' brief, she was equally terse and abruptly ended the call. Back to the drawing board, and after a phone around I eventually got one.

I wondered how many empty seats there would be amongst the home fans since it was all Gers supporters as I approached the stadium and I was soon renewing a few old acquaintances. No way could I have gone in the wrong end.

After taking a few photographs, kept on the lookout for programme sellers but to no avail, so I joined the slow-moving queue at my designated turnstile. The electronic entry procedure caught me by surprise and I fumbled around, inserting and removing the ticket a few times before the green light indicated that I could pass. This system

The Saints go marching on!

should be more efficient than, say, the chap with the wads of cash controlling the turnstiles at the home of the Blue Brazil, but I actually think it slowed things down and wondered how the elderly or people with impairments would find it.

Inside, I got my bearings and located the programme vendor, toilets and snack bar. There was a hot dog stall and a great selection of pies and pastries which you could supplement with baked beans. The fans were being offered much more choice than usual – and it looked as though they were lapping it up. After our big breakfast I wasn't hungry and, missing out on what looked like good grub, I purchased a Bovril (£1.70) and a shiny programme (£2.50) before heading out into the sunshine.

The first thing that struck me was how good the pitch looked. I thought it was artificial turf, but this was just a strip around the perimeter. The grass playing surface was almost like a carpet. That should help with the quality of the football, I thought. The stadium itself was compact with four all-seated stands, but no terracing. Everything seemed well organised and there was a good mix of stewards and police officers.

My front row pew was right next to the entrance from the concourse, and I soon got annoyed by the constant comings and goings. This sort of thing wouldn't have been as much of an issue on a terrace. At least I was close to the action and sat back in anticipation as the teams lined up across at the tunnel.

Formalities over, the game got under way without as much as a peep from the 5,000-plus crowd. It was all Rangers, the Saints just making up the numbers. This was the top playing the bottom, and it showed. The football was nothing to shout about, which might explain why there was very little shouting coming from the stands. The bigger club took the lead and with St Mirren's game all but over, half time was upon us. It was good to get a chance to move around for a while and heat up a bit.

During the break there was some entertainment, which passed the time. However the atmosphere was definitely flat, the main reason being the lack of competition on the field. I have no doubt that the majority of the fans expected a Rangers victory and I personally don't think this level of predictability is healthy for the Scottish game: there's far too big a gap between the Old Firm and the rest. Radical action is required to make the SPL more competitive (and that will remain the case, whatever the outcome of Rangers 2012 crisis).

In the second half, Rangers continued to dominate and scored another couple of goals, one of which was excellent. The Saints did get a consolation and threatened for a few minutes, but overall their resistance was weak. The ref made a few unusual decisions and was ridiculed by all and sundry. Five minutes before the end, the crowd started to disperse.

St Mirren have been on sale since 2009 and a deal involving the supporters has been bubbling below the surface for some time. It now looks likely to come to fruition and the supporters will have a say in how the club is run. The stadium and surrounding facilities are in place, the club have SPL status and have enjoyed reasonable cup runs in recent seasons. However, for any club, is there any point being in a league they have no chance of winning? Wouldn't it be more interesting and exciting to have a chance of real success, rather than survival being considered an achievement in itself? It can't be easy for St Mirren fans, making up the numbers week after week and hoping to avoid defeat. In my opinion, the SPL needs to be more like the championship in England where numerous teams can potentially win the league – which takes us back to the Old Firm question. However desirable, a Rangers and Celtic migration to the English Premier League is not on the cards, or at least, not as yet. So what's the alternative?

The current 12-team top division must be expanded. It's boring playing the same teams at least four times a season, so why not add another couple of teams, play each other home and away and then split top and bottom for another six games. OK, its still highly unlikely that the Saints could win the league but they could be competing for a European place or to avoid the dreaded relegation or play-offs that would result from finishing lower down the league. The type of format I'm suggesting means fewer meaningless games and excitement right to the end of the season – the English championship play-offs are testament to this. Two up two down, thirds playing off against each other, whatever, there are many exciting permutations and there's no doubt clubs like St Mirren would benefit.

Quote of the day – *Catering attendant to startled fan: 'Do you want beans wi' yer pie?' Fan: 'Beans?' Obviously he'd never been asked that question at a football match in Scotland before.*

GAME	ST MIRREN VERSUS RANGERS
DIVISION	SPL
DATE	SUN 7 NOV 2010, KO 12PM
VENUE	ST MIRREN PARK, ATTENDANCE 5,674
SCORE	1-3

MATCH STATS:
HTTP://WWW.SCOTPREM.COM/CONTENT/DEFAULT.ASP?PAGE=S29_1_1
&WORKINGDATE=2010-11-7

14

THE DIAMONDS V LIVI LIONS

A Programme to Remember

THE EXCELSIOR STADIUM in Airdrie was my destination for the Irn-Bru Division Two clash with Livingston. There was a furore when it opened as the Shyberry Excelsior and I'd been of the understanding that they'd renamed it New Broomfield. Now, just to confuse matters, my car park ticket carried an advert for 'Airdrie Football Centre @ Broomfield Stadium'.

I'd been to 'old' Broomfield years ago and vividly recalled the raucous atmosphere and the sense of closeness to the players on the pitch. How would the new stadium compare?

Outside the Main Stand, lots of kids were running around wearing club tracksuits, the club shop was busy, stewards were directing people to their desired destinations and there was a sponsored white van, liveried with the colours and emblems of Airdrie United, all of which suggested good links with the local community. The main sign still read AUFC rather than AFC. I couldn't help feeling it was all a bit of a shame really. Why couldn't we just revert back to Airdrieonians Football Club and get on with it. Does it really matter?

While looking for a turnstile, I noticed that the lounge bar appeared to be open to anyone. Yes, you can get a pint before a game at the Excelsior. If only I hadn't been driving.

As no vendors were in sight, I headed for the club shop where £2 got me the 'Lest We Forget' programme with the now infamous front cover picture of German soldiers on a train – definitely one Remembrance Sunday tribute that we will never forget. At the entrance I tendered a £20 note to the chap behind the grille with the Blue Brazil pile in his hand (St Mirren's automated system, in hindsight, now seemed very transparent and efficient) and received a fiver change, then set off into the concourse. As at several other venues, I noticed underutilised areas, and once more it struck me that there could, and should be more going on for the fans, not only on match days. Too few of the clubs are optimising use of the facilities outwith football matches.

The Excelsior has four good, all-seated stands (those on either side of the goals were netted off on the day of my visit), a fantastic looking pitch (which I later realised was artificial turf) and two electronic scoreboards, which were somewhat hidden in the depths of the goal end sections. Overall, a very impressive facility, supplemented by numerous artificial pitches on the perimeter – just what I like to see at a football club.

The PA was blaring out 'Only the Lonely' – and to me the song title was spot-on, given the disappointing turnout of 1,013. Teams out and a minute's silence, impeccably observed. Then the usual jeers and cheers as the game got under way. I was convinced that the excellent playing surface was promoting a better playing style – the football authorities must make it a priority to evaluate the benefits artificial turf might bring to the game as a whole. Henry McLeish is complimentary about them in his official review and the games I've seen to date on the 3/4G have been better – I don't think that's a coincidence.

The skinny young Airdrie boys started the better team but Livingston got a foothold and went on to dominate proceedings. Both teams played a fast, passing game that was competitive without being dirty. As a nation, we continually roar at our teams to get up the park, irrespective of how they get there, and this is one of the reasons we fail at higher levels. Livingston perfectly illustrated the value of the opposite tactics, choosing their moments to up the tempo. Meanwhile, the home side were continually being urged up the park by their coaching staff and captain, and they demonstrated no patience, no composure, no stealthy build-up.

Where every club should be

At half time I headed downstairs to purchase my lunch. I spotted a space and manoeuvred through the Diamonds faithful to the border shelf where I thoroughly enjoyed my steak pie and Bovril (best yet) and mulled over the strange transactions that had been going on between the catering staff and the teenagers in the club tracksuits.

There were posters dotted around the ground advertising the local newspaper as 'the heart and soul of the community', a slogan that I would like to see applying universally to all Scottish football clubs in celebration of the part they play in enhancing their locality. It

There appears to be a 'U' missing?

would certainly seem that Airdrie United are doing just that. Floodlights on, and another interesting jostle in the second half. Livingston got their break and scored after a swift move. The Airdire fans might have had it that Lady Luck wasn't on their side, but it wasn't a matter of luck: Livingston could point to the game plan they adopted and, more importantly, stuck to. Game over.

The car park was emptying slowly and I wondered if parking there had been the right option because the main road was littered with vehicles whose drivers had decided against paying the parking fee. But in hindsight, it was much better value than £5 Livingston charge and all very easy for travelling supporters. On the cold, dark road home, I made the comparison with the early kick offs on the past two Sundays. By now they were definitely my preferred option.

I had thoroughly enjoyed my day. There was something very traditional about Airdrie that I liked and the Excelsior had a bit of character. Maybe it was the Bentley parked outside the Main Stand or the cameraderie between the people associated with the club – perhaps the recent turmoil had brought them that bit closer together. Who knows, but there was definitely something going for the Diamonds. As to the future, an excellent infrastructure is in place and there is plenty potential for development. On the downside, they are bang in the middle of the Central Belt, close to the Glasgow giants and surrounded by other provincial clubs – too many, in my opinion – and this means they will find it very difficult to increase their fan base.

The one advantage they have over their local rivals Albion Rovers and Motherwell is that their complex boasts modern, accessible facilities that promote more than just football. The club website showcases the Excelsior's business, conference and function suites and executive boxes. As a football centre they offer state-of-the-art facilities – you can even hire the main pitch. Youth teams, a ladies' team and a supporters' trust are all in place. The club appear to be doing all they can in the current context and I'm sure they would grasp any opportunity to fulfil their potential.

Quote of the day – *'Only the Lonely' sung by Roy Orbison, sadly appropriate.*

GAME	AIRDRIE UNITED VERSUS LIVINGSTON
DIVISION	SFL2
DATE	SAT 13 NOV 2010, KO 3PM
VENUE	EXCELSIOR STADIUM, ATTENDANCE 1,013
SCORE	0-1

MATCH STATS:
HTTP://WWW.SCOTTISHFOOTBALLLEAGUE.COM/FOOTBALL/SECOND/
RESULTS/3283487/

15

THE WASPS V THE ROVERS

Standing Ovation

THIS WAS THE FIRST time I had attended a game in the Scottish Cup in the year before the Final – previously it has always been third round onwards, and then the Cup Final itself, one of my favourite football days – it's always good to end the season with the showpiece game, especially if your own team wins. Keen to choose a competitive match rather than a senior team against some minnow, I decided on Alloa v Raith, having briefly pondered Peterhead again (I couldn't hack the ten-hour round trip).

On the road to Alloa, I completely missed the cut-off for the M876 – I blame *Off the Ball* – and the gloom was fast descending as I approached Recreation Park. There seemed to be a stand missing, which may have had something to do with the fairly new railway line that ran alongside the ground. From the outside, the place looked more like a builder's yard than anything else. At least there was a fenced, five-a-side, all-weather pitch (better than nothing). The fixed signage at the home entrance displayed 'Adults £10', which was at variance with temporary signs displaying 'Adults £13' – what a great way to endear the club to supporters (especially away ones). How much would it be if the Old Firm were in town? I chose the turnstile next to the entrance for players and officials, pushed £13 through a small square hole and entered. What a place! Central Park, home of

Alloa, Alloa

the Blue Brazil, had been the worst ground I'd experienced to date. This place was vying with Cowdenbeath for worst senior ground in Scotland. Recreation Park was a combination of grass embankments, temporary covered seating, a concrete terrace and an old Main Stand with a standing area below which felt like being in a garage – a far cry from what you might be entitled to expect in modern-day Scotland. On the plus side, it did have a homely feel and you could sense the club's connection with the local community (something lacking at too many other clubs). Programme purchased, I sampled a steak pie (not very good) and Bovril (best yet). The snack bar menu was slightly more expansive than normal. Supplementing the usual dross were 'home-made' lentil soup and stovies, which added to the homely appeal of Alloa Athletic.

As I was making my way to the Main Stand, I noticed a sign announcing that I would have to pay another pound to sit there. Not today, I thought, and decided to give the official standing area a try. Even although I was freezing cold by the time the final whistle went, it was nice to have the option to stand. This is something the big clubs should consider offering the fans, authorities agreeing of course.

Floodlights on, and we're off. The First Division visitors dominated the early stages, much to the delight of the travelling support, and they deserved their lead. I was enjoying my touchline position. In the crowd there were families huddled together (one with a baby), groups of mates and the usual gang of feral teenagers. Lots of people were openly smoking – since we were in the open air, I had no problem with that. A noisy goods train rolled by at the grassy stand end and there was generally loads of other things going on – oh, and the football as well. When you're not seated, your focus definitely wanders. But it was a good game and the artificial surface looked great to play on.

Homely fare

At half time, incredibly, the home side were 2-1 up, thanks to two goals in two minutes. Also, the visitors had a player sent off a minute before the break – game on for the Wasps. I went over to the concrete terrace in the hope that moving about would warm me up (those balmy afternoons at the start of the season were by now a distant memory), and took some photographs of the ramshackle buildings and other components collectively known as Recreation Park. Major works would be required to bring the place up to a reasonable standard.

In the second half, the home team continued their forays towards the opposition goal and with Raith Rovers still trying, it made for a really entertaining game. The stand-side linesman constantly encouraged the players to play the game properly and the atmosphere was all very positive – why does this sort of thing never get reported in the media?

Alloa dominated the rest of the proceedings with an outstanding performance and a hat-trick from Kevin McDonald. I was only glad to hear the final whistle because by then it was bitterly cold and the rain was turning to hail. Time for the road. I headed back, 'Don't Stop Believing' ringing in my ears (all the kids were singing it).

I had thoroughly enjoyed my day. I really like the community atmosphere at the smaller clubs – the home-made stovies, the families on an outing, the sense of local community. Today's game was good, but I was beginning to wonder if that was the most important thing.

As for so many other provincial clubs, the Wasps' future is precarious. Their lack of facilities is an obvious problem, but not an insurmountable one, and the low average attendance is a challenge. At Alloa there are good foundations to build on and with some smart professional management I'm convinced the Wasps could prosper. It would be good to ask the fans and other local people to come up with ideas to progress the club and let the management improve both the club and the general community. Some blue-sky thinking is required for Scottish football as a whole.

Quote of the day – *Man in the Gents: 'Building sites have better toilets.'*

GAME	ALLOA ATHLETIC VERSUS RAITH ROVERS
DIVISION	SCR3
DATE	SAT 20 NOV 2010. KO 3PM
VENUE	RECREATION PARK, ATTENDANCE 1,039
SCORE	4-2

MATCH STATS:
HTTP://WWW.SCOTTISHFA.CO.UK/SCOTTISH_CUP_FIXTURE_DETAILS.CFM?PAGE=1988&MATCHID=104261

16

KILLIE V THE DONS

Referee, Is the Baw Burst?

WHAT A WEEK it's been for Scottish football. A referees' strike, officials and administrators sacked and general mayhem throughout the game. But never mind, it's Saturday again. Back to 'reality' and the fitba'. Only six games to choose from the SPL over Saturday and Sunday due to the refs' strike and the weather. My most realistic options were Hamilton or Kilmarnock. It was another fine, albeit bitterly cold, winter's day and I decided to choose my local SPL team on the basis that it would be easy to get there and back if the weather turned nasty.

I had been to Rugby Park before as a visiting supporter so knew roughly what to expect and where to go. I headed for the main entrance to take some photographs and sample the pre-match atmosphere. There was plenty going on at the Sports Bar and at the adjacent Park Hotel, with loads of people hanging around outside despite the cold. It was good that you could get a drink before the match if you fancied one. I don't know how busy the bars were and how easy it would be to get served, probably easier than at the pubs around Hampden I suspect. There was no drunken or loutish behaviour whatsoever, which highlights the fact that we can have a few before a game and still behave in a responsible manner.

On my way back round to the Moffat Stand I noticed a sign saying that Killie were the oldest professional club in Scotland. That got me thinking. I was of the opinion that Queen's Park were the oldest and wondered if it was something to do with amateur status, were Killie professional from day one – could be interesting? In through the turnstile and back to the premium prices of the Premier League – £20 for admission. Add the cost of the programme (£2.50), a pie and Bovril (£3.70) and travel, and my expenses for the day crossed the £30 mark – and this was effectively a home game.

The admission fee is my biggest gripe, particularly for SPL games –

Back in '69, 1869 that is!

basically, you're paying approximately £15 an hour for the pleasure. I think that the clubs should make a ceiling for the spend per individual, and this should include ticket, programme, refreshments and raffle tickets.

Right, ten minutes to kick off and it's time to sample the famous Killie pie (which turns out not to be the best pie I've tasted this season). Recently I've been eating pre-match rather than at half time, basically because I wasn't eating my evening meal. When you think about it, 4-ish is a bit late for a hearty snack. Is 3pm the right time to be kicking off a football match? Has society and the supporter now moved away from the traditional kick-off time? My view is that a rethink is required.

The teams ran out onto a frosty looking grass surface. Artificial turf is a must. I would have thought that with so many games being off, some 'loose end' supporters would have turned up to swell the ranks of the spectators, but the turnout was really disappointing. Maybe the weather put people off, or maybe it's just so much easier to stand in a pub.

The Israeli ref blew his whistle and the game was under way in front of the paltry crowd. Both teams started somewhat gingerly – conditions underfoot might well have had something to do with this. The visitors seemed to lack direction and purpose (as they had all season). Kilmarnock started dominating proceedings and took the lead. No real surprises there. Things were looking good both for the locals and my coupon.

Half time, and my main objective was to try and heat up. The football had been OK but certainly not enough to get you out of the seat and jumping around, so the atmosphere had been pretty flat throughout. The Dons fans were scarce and predictably quiet. All in all, it was quite a sombre experience.

At the back of the stand a lengthy queue formed for the snack bars and without doubt some unlucky supporters were going miss some of the second half. This is such a common situation in so many Scottish grounds, and yet surely better service would mean winners all round – moving goods more quickly surely making more money.

Back at my seat, I took a look through the programme but found nothing much of interest. Killie continued to dominate in the second half, with Eremenko pulling strings in midfield. They got a second goal and the game was effectively over after an hour. The rest of the afternoon was spent watching some good passing moves and trying to keep warm. Many fans left before the final whistle and I was tempted, but I was there for the review and was therefore committed to staying to the end. I was bitterly cold by the time I headed for the car, asking myself the usual questions. Why was it a no-show for so many fans? Why have games in deepest, darkest winter? Why have a mid-afternoon kick off as standard for weekend games? Why persevere with grass playing surfaces? Fundamental change will be required to ensure the future of Scottish football. Are we ready for it and what is the consensus?

As for Kilmarnock, an SPL club heavily in debt with no noticeable training facilities and, more worryingly, no obvious ambition – the future is a concern. This club should be a shining light in the Scottish game – they have the history, the stadium (albeit one-dimensional) and no serious competition close by. Much as I was impressed with the club, they are nowhere near their potential – change is required.

Roll the clocks forward 18 months and the situation has changed. Killie have just lifted the League Cup,

Past glories

overcoming Celtic in the final, they've beaten Rangers home and away in the league and are top of the 'bottom' six. Club chairman Michael Johnston is talking about Scottish football's Arab Spring as ten of the 12 SPL clubs (Celtic and Rangers not invited) met to discuss the voting structure. Johnston told the BBC, 'There's definitely a mood for change and, if we're going to have radical change, then there has to be a more flexible voting structure… Anything that makes the smaller clubs more competitive is going to lead to a better competition and hopefully make it a better viewing spectacle for Sky, ESPN and the BBC.' My sentiments exactly. At last something is happening and people are challenging the status quo. Johnston also stated: 'Make the league more competitive.' I couldn't agree more. As well as achieving enhanced attendance figures, it would mean a better product to take to the TV companies who are currently dictating what everyone and their granny should do. Fingers crossed that Scottish football's Arab Spring is, at long last, under way.

Quote of the day – *Kilmarnock fan, 'Referee's a wanker.' No matter where there from, who they are or what they do – the refereeing fraternity are always on the losing side.*

GAME	KILMARNOCK VERSUS ABERDEEN
DIVISION	SPL
DATE	SAT 27 NOV 2010, KO 3PM
VENUE	RUGBY PARK, ATTENDANCE 5,013
SCORE	2-0

MATCH STATS:
HTTP://WWW.SCOTPREM.COM/CONTENT/DEFAULT.ASP?PAGE=S26_1_1 &WORKINGDATE=2010-11-27

17

THE PARS V THE DOONHAMERS

No Steak Pies Here, We're Fifers!

AFTER TWO WEEKS of chaos due to the weather, summer football suddenly seemed very appealing. Even though the 'big thaw' had taken place, the football card had been decimated again. Today's choices were Dunfermline or East Fife, selected because they are close to each other – one might have been called off at the last minute. There were other potential matches in the SPL (Inverness, which I'd scheduled for during the holidays), Division One (Morton or Partick, quite close to home so I was keeping these ones up my sleeve) and Peterhead or Montrose (too far away). So, East End Park it was for my first visit since around 2002 when Dunfermline were an SPL club and probably doing as well as they had done since the '60s. The two Jimmys were in residence, with a certain Ian Ferguson (one of Scotland's most decorated players) as captain. Changed days indeed.

North of the Kincardine Bridge the temperature dropped and although the weather hadn't changed dramatically, the landscape did – I was amazed by the amount of snow piled high at the roadside and blanketing the fields. My thoughts rewound to Monday, when I had been stuck on the M80 for four hours, before reversing off the motorway and making it into Stirling to spend the night in a hotel – and I was one of the lucky ones.

I was soon crawling through the traffic in Dunfermline town centre. Any idea that it might be so busy because of the match was wishful thinking: it was the Christmas shoppers. What would you rather do, go shopping or go to the football? It's a no-brainer as far as I'm concerned – what is it about shopping? Anyway, after a 15-minute hold-up I was headed down to the free car park at Leys Park Road. This is where the trouble began. Just as I turned off the roundabout, the policewoman directing the traffic informed me that the car park was full but to carry

There never used to be a Munro here!

on and turn around. Unfortunately, I was unable to turn because of the congestion and I found myself in the snow-covered car park where, despite what I'd been told, I managed to find a space. I skidded my way into it with some help from a couple of Pars fans and the shovel I had in the boot. By now it was 2.55 and it looked as if I was going to miss the start of the game as I trudged through the snow and over towards the wall at the end of the cul-de-sac that leads onto Halbeath Road. Someone had decided to pile a small mountain of snow there and the supporters were really struggling to get over it. Should this game really have gone ahead, I wondered, as I slithered down onto the icy pavement – this was really treacherous.

Got there in the end though. At the entrance to the Norrie McCathie Stand, a steward clad in the standard yellow hi-viz jacket was informing everyone that there would not be any catering in the stand, so I enquired about the Main Stand arrangements. Much to my relief, she confirmed that there was a cash turnstile and that food was available there. Programme in hand, I made for my seat. The game was already under way – the Pars v the Doonhamers for the second time this season – a top of the table clash. Despite my high hopes, the quality of the football was terrible. The game was very scrappy. I suffered until 3.20 before heading down below to find the snack bar.

I wondered if the recent long lay-off had affected the teams, the players looked so lethargic. The pitch looked OK, certainly in the first half, and the weather wasn't too cold, so what was wrong?

There was no queue at the snack bar to delay gratification. Paying no attention to the menu suspended above the counter, I asked for a steak pie and a Bovril. The server was a little bemused by my request for a steak pie and I had to repeat the sentence. 'Steak bridie,' she corrected me, looking at me as if I was from another planet. I reminded myself I was in Fife.

Back in the stand, I devoured the largest steak offering of the season to date and thoroughly enjoyed my hot and tasty Bovril. The first half dragged to a close with hardly a whimper from the supporters. There was no atmosphere whatsoever, even though their team could go top today. I had yet to see or hear any supporters from Dumfries, which was disappointing, but what about the Pars fans, where were they? Just over 2,000 had made it to see the team go top.

The half-time break was spent checking scores for the coupon, browsing through the programme and trying to keep warm. It was getting darker by the second and freezing fog was enveloping the stadium. I started thinking about my precarious parking place. The thought of exiting the car park was worrying me and so I decided to leave a wee bit early rather than get stuck for ages and be even later home – the wife would not be pleased, particularly when *Strictly* and *X Factor* were into the finals.

The second half was much more entertaining than the first and both teams played some decent football. Dunfermline started to get a grip on the game and were edging the proceedings on the rapidly deteriorating pitch – artificial turf is a must, I'm now completely convinced. Even so, there was still not much noise from the crowd and I wondered if this was as good as it gets from Dunfermline's point of view. My thoughts on the Old Firm leaving Scotland were primarily driven by the boost the other clubs would get by creating a more challenging and balanced league (which we already have in Divisions One, Two and Three). But now I was asking myself, would it really make a difference for the other SPL clubs?

Half chances at either end were at last warming the fans up a touch. However, there was little to suggest that the game would finish with a winner and I made my exit just after 4.30. It felt strange to leave before the final whistle, something I haven't done in years, but it was necessary. Unfortunately, I missed both the sending-off and the late goal for the hosts, but to be honest I was fed up and was glad to be on my way. The car park wasn't as difficult to exit as I had feared and I was soon on my way.

There was a lot to mull over on the drive south, the paltry crowd, for one thing. Sure, it was getting close to Christmas and times were tough, but that was a pathetic turn-out for a team pushing for promotion. Dumfries isn't exactly a small town either, where were the Doonhamers faithful? Or could such low attendance figures have something to do with scheduling football matches in deepest, darkest winter?

On my way into the stadium I had noticed hospitality prices starting at £15 – cheaper than what I paid to get in, so it's obvious that the club are trying hard to get the much-needed corporate monies. However, £16 was a bit steep for a 'normal' supporter and I wondered if the club might be able to reduce the admission price for the average fan. Ticket prices are definitely something that has to be reviewed. Throw in the programme, food and drink, and fuel, and you're looking at £30 for an afternoon's entertainment for one person. I could take the better half to the movies for much less, and that includes her nibbles, which can be pricey.

In the Second and Third Divisions I think they've got the pricing structure right: £10–£12 for the ticket represents good value for 90 minutes of football. But for the higher leagues, it is way over the top – no way is the football that much better, nor are most of the stadiums, so how can it be justified?

Quote of the day – Me: *'Steak pie please?' Bewildered look from server It's a bridie, yer in Fife, I reminded myself.*

GAME	DUNFERMLINE VERSUS QUEEN OF THE SOUTH
DIVISION	SFL1
DATE	SAT 11 DEC 2010, KO 3PM
VENUE	EAST END PARK, ATTENDANCE 2,062
SCORE	1-0

MATCH STATS:
HTTP://WWW.SCOTTISHFOOTBALLLEAGUE.COM/FOOTBALL/FIRST/
RESULTS/3283730/

18

THE ACCIES V THE DONS

Don Over

HAMILTON WAS THE DESTINATION, for a bottom of the table scrap with lowly Aberdeen. It was good to be going to the football again after an enforced break due to the weather. I'm now firmly in the 'summer' football camp and the sooner we sort this out the better. It will be a fundamental shift, and a risky one. But swift, decisive change is needed. In fact, each and every avenue should be explored to get more fans back to the football – this must be the primary objective for all the clubs and the powers that be.

The majority of the options for today's football were at night, and some grounds had already been visited, so I decided on New Douglas Park. Evening games, particularly after work, have never been high on my agenda and the thought of heading out on a cold winter's night to get even colder was not at all appealing. A Celtic game the week before was played in temperatures around minus five. Some of the comments I heard on radio shows were ridiculous – 'The players will warm up quickly, they are desperate for a game' was definitely the most annoying. Fine, but what about the fans sitting in the freezing cold and dealing with terrible road and pavement conditions to get to the game?

The first thing I noticed on arriving at New Douglas Park was the amount of Aberdeen supporters. They certainly made their presence known during the match. I thought of the significant contribution that they must make to the Accies' coffers – Scottish football needs a strong Aberdeen.

I carried on round to the Accies end. Underneath the Main Stand there were shops, offices and even a nursery. Maximising the use of the premises can only benefit clubs, and here it was evidently being done well.

Old gates at New Douglas

I hurried round past the main entrance to the far corner, dodged all the fans coming from the nearby Hamilton West station (there are great transport links to New Douglas Park) and entered a turnstile. The young attendant asked whether I was 'adult or junior'. 'Thanks for the compliment!' was my reply as I handed her a crisp £20 note. On entering the stadium you are still outside and almost pitch-side, which I like, it adds to the feeling that you're close to the action. I purchased my programme from the vendor in the 'mini garden shed' and at the snack bar I selected my usual fare, steak pie (£2.10) and Bovril (£1.70), from the smallest menu to date – modern stadium and facilities, yet ancient catering standards. The food and drink were OK though.

Both teams started at a reasonable pace. The pitch looked good and it was pleasing to be able to hear absolutely everything. Now I know you can hear a lot more at the smaller stadiums but for some reason it was more striking than usual. The atmosphere was mostly down to the Aberdeen fans who were fairly raucous throughout. The same couldn't be said of the home lot. To be fair, there wasn't much for them to shout about. The youngish looking Hamilton side probably edged the early stages. Aberdeen, under the new management of Brown and Knox, gradually got a grip of things and finished the first half the stronger side. The ref's half-time whistle was a relief as I was desperate to stand up and try and generate some heat. Many of the fans surrounding me were evidently of the same opinion. Again, I thought about the all-seated stadium criteria – is it really necessary?

During the break I read the entire programme (that gives you an idea of the quality) and took in my surroundings. There were a lot of families among the home support and many of the youngsters were kitted out in the clubs tracksuits. All good stuff. I got the impression

Looks comfy in there!

that Hamilton were evolving, there was just something about the place, something that gave me that optimistic feeling. The area surrounding the stadium had been significantly developed in recent years and the club sat well within it. Pity about the football.

The second half was much better than the first. The home team had a real go, all credit to them. A 0-0 score started to look on the cards, but the managers weren't happy to settle for that and both made a number of substitutions. Hamilton continued to push forward but real chances were few and far between. With the 90 minutes over and the board showing two minutes' added time, Hamilton surged forward, only to be thwarted and then hit by a swift counter-attack. Aberdeen scored. Was this to be a defining moment in Hamilton's season? I hoped not, as I had enjoyed my first outing to their home ground and would definitely be back.

As the mass exodus started, the Aberdeen players and some fans celebrated on the pitch. I joined the New Douglas Park faithful and made my exit into the gloomy evening, passing the noisy Spice of Life Stand on my way back to the car.

That result represented a killer blow for Hamilton and another three points for the Dons' new management team – two wins in a row. I'd thought the Aberdeen side I had seen at Kilmarnock a few weeks ago was poor and to be honest there wasn't much difference today, apart from luck, but that's football for you.

Exiting the car park was easy and I was soon heading for the A725 and thick fog. It had been a long winter and it wasn't not even January yet. Is playing through the worst winter months really necessary? In a word, no. March to November seems more sensible to me and it appears that some in the corridors of power are finally waking up to the idea. SFA president Campbell Ogilvie says it is time for the country to take the idea of switching to a summer game seriously. He cites the improvement in the women's game as evidence of the benefits and takes the view that all youth and professional youth football should follow suit. Premier League managers, including Peter Houston, Kenny Shiels and Danny Lennon have told the BBC that they are in favour of a switch, as is Sheila Begbie, the SFA head of women's and girls' football.

Need I say more? Can we end this winter misery once and for all?

Quote of the day – *Hamilton fan: 'Has yer erm thawed oot yit, linesman?'*

GAME	HAMILTON VERSUS ABERDEEN
DIVISION	SPL
DATE	WED 29 DEC 2010, KO 3PM
VENUE	NEW DOUGLAS PARK, ATTENDANCE 2,968
SCORE	0-1

MATCH STATS:
HTTP://WWW.SCOTPREM.COM/CONTENT/DEFAULT.ASP?PAGE=S23_I_I
&WORKINGDATE=2010-12-29

19

THE HIBEES V THE HONEST MEN

Officer: 'I'm an Honest Man, honestly.'

GAME 19 BECKONED and again bad weather was playing havoc with the fixture list. My desired options diminished considerably as the call-offs (Albion, Dumbarton and Falkirk) mounted during the week leaving only one suitable but intriguing game – Hibernian v Ayr United in the fourth round of the Scottish Cup.

I set off for Leith, blissfully unaware of the treacherous driving conditions that I would soon encounter – no more arguments from me, it's fair-weather football and the sooner the better. As I headed inland, conditions steadily deteriorated with sleet, snow and ice causing problems. It crossed my mind that I should I just turn back, but having missed so many games recently it wasn't an option if I was to fulfil my aim of getting round all the grounds in one season. I passed a car upside down on the hard shoulder, saw another in a field (how on earth it got in there I will never know), and several at the side of the road with hazard warning lights on – it was madness, but I got through it and eventually found myself in deepest Leith.

I had been listening to *Off the Ball* and there was a feeling that there could be an upset at Easter Road today. I thought back to Game 1 at Somerset Park in sunny August, and recalled how vulnerable I thought Ayr United would be this season. What a difference a few months can make – and all credit to them for turning around a poor start and placing themselves into contention for promotion. As for Hibs, what a contrast. I had been impressed after watching them in the very entertaining game at Fir Park where they won 3-2, but they had slipped alarmingly into the relegation zone, got a new manager and sold one of their top players to Celtic – it's amazing how quickly things change in football.

I turned off Easter Road into St Clair Street and after a few U-turns

Cold and quiet at Easter Road

was lucky enough to get a space on St Clair Avenue. Typically, it was at the opposite end of the ground from where I was intending to join up with the fans from my local 'wee' team, the so-called Honest Men of Ayr United. With plenty of time to spare, I approached the stadium for my first visit in over 20 years. My memories of the old Easter Road were not favourable – I recalled a shabby stadium surrounded by crumbling housing and dilapidated industrial buildings. The whole area has changed considerably for the better, and nothing more than the stadium itself. Good on the engineers for designing something that had to be built in such a restricted space. There were still some traces of the past but generally there was a modern, vibrant buzz.

Outside the Famous Five Stand, I made a beeline for one of the hi-viz brigade who directed me to the South Stand at the other end of the stadium and explained the procedure for gaining entry. I trotted off past the club shop, ticket office and various sets of green gates, taking some photos on the way, until I reached the portacabin/shed on Albion Road where I purchased my 'sit anywhere' ticket. I then entered through one of the tightest turnstiles yet (I know the festive season was just over, but the belly hadn't increased that much) handed over the ticket, which I thought was all a bit pointless (ticket office and

Wish they were playing

turnstile overheads) and walked into the spacious concourse. Plenty of room for a bar, I thought. The atmosphere was already building. Lots of shouting and singing filled the air but unfortunately it was getting out of hand and some of the Honest Men from my neck of the woods were refused entry due to their over-excited, inebriated state.

At the snack bar, 'Today's Menu' was ever so slightly more expansive than the choice offered at most Scottish football grounds. I was now accustomed to my weekly intake of stodge and wondered if I should continue down the pie and Bovril road – what else did I really like though?

With kick-off time approaching, I headed out into the floodlit arena in the lower tier of the South Stand. The place was busy with rowdy Ayr fans, which was good to an extent as there was a decent level of noise in the stadium. Unfortunately, there was little or no noise coming from the other three stands. This emphasises how important away fans are to a game of football – every effort should be made to encourage them to come along.

Teams out, floodlights blazing and game on at a half-empty Easter Road. This surprised me somewhat, as I imagined Hibs and Hearts would be playing to almost full houses every other week in the Scottish Capital. A measly 6,065 people had turned up for the game, with a good 500 or so from Ayrshire. Surely the Hibees could have enticed more fans to the match? Easier said than done, given that the quality on show was pretty awful. Hibs were a shadow of the team that I had watched at Fir Park and their lacklustre display eventually let Ayr get a foothold. There was nothing much to shout about in the first half, but the Ayr United fans were determined to put on their own show for Lothian and Borders' finest. For whatever reason, a section of Honest Men were drunk, abusive and generally intent on winding up everyone without a black and white scarf on, and they were succeeding. A number of cautions were issued by stewards and police officers before the inevitable arrests were made. The dissent continued throughout the match and at one stage a powerful flare lit up the South Stand and filled the air with smoke. What was going on?

The second half brought a few chances at either end, but still nothing to shout about. The pitch seemed to be holding out and the Ayr fans had calmed down as well, possibly due to the cold that was setting in and even though many of them had been on their feet throughout the entire match.

Both managers made substitutions in order to freshen things up but real chances were almost non-existent. I suddenly had a horrible thought: will this game go to extra time? I would have asked the gentlemen next to me but they were continuously sipping from hip flasks (like many others) and probably wouldn't have had a clue. I made up my mind that it would go to a replay and counted down the minutes with frequent backward glances to the scoreboard. One last chance for the visitors was missed and as soon as the ref brought proceedings to halt I made a sharp exit.

My haste was to no avail and I struggled against the throng all the way back to the Famous Five Stand – I wished they had been playing. I slipped and skidded back to the car and was soon on the road west, glad that I had ticked the second Edinburgh box.

I was troubled by several aspects of the game – from the size of the crowd, to the behaviour of my country cousins, to the poor quality of the football. Hibernian are one of the country's biggest clubs, they are based in a vibrant, cosmopolitan city, so why the lack of interest in the beautiful game? OK, I know rugby is big in these parts, but surely the modern set-up and history of the club should be appealing to more people? Why sit and watch Sky television when you could sample the real thing? Why watch the English Premiership in the boozer, coupon in hand, rather than be at the football?

I know there are arguments about the quality (or lack of) of the game compared to what's on offer on the other side of Hadrian's Wall but I'm not convinced. Take away the top six in the EPL and you have some major dross in there – it's all about marketing. Here in Scotland we need to promote our game better.

As I crawled through the Edinburgh traffic, I thought back to my Tynecastle visit and the problems I experienced getting to and from the stadium. This is a real dilemma for clubs: do we move to modern, generally more accessible stadiums, or remain at the heart of the communities where the clubs were born? I would always prefer the latter, as the thought of walking to the game, where possible, is more 'natural'. But in this season's journey I have found that the out-of-town stadiums are much easier to get to, particularly by car. Perhaps Hearts should take note.

Quote of the day – *Ayr United fan: 'That would have been in if it wisnae for that goalie.'*

GAME	HIBERNIAN VERSUS AYR UNITED
DIVISION	SCR4
DATE	SAT 8 JAN 2011, KO 3PM
VENUE	EASTER ROAD, ATTENDANCE 6,065
SCORE	0-0

MATCH STATS:
HTTP://WWW.SCOTTISHFA.CO.UK/SCOTTISH_CUP_FIXTURE_DETAILS.
CFM?PAGE=1988&MATCHID=105278

20

THE DEE V THE WELL

Stadium Deelema

TWO GAMES IN TWO DAYS, my wife and family think I'm mad. Now for another Scottish Cup encounter, Dundee v Motherwell at Dens Park. The appalling weather was still with us but an overnight stay in Glasgow meant there was not as far to travel to the City of Discovery. I was a bit late leaving the west end and there were nightmare driving conditions with the A9 down to one lane from Dunblane to Perth. Time was marching on and I thought about turning back, but I decided to plod on and was eventually on the Kingsway with about 15 minutes to spare before kick off. I knew roughly where Dens Park was and that the stadium would be signposted, so no need for the SatNav. Or so I thought. I took a wrong turning, lost my bearings and had to stop and fire up the old navigation system: it displayed five minutes to Tannadice Street. After whizzing along some back roads that were totally covered in snow, I parked outside the snooker club in Dundonald Street and hastily made my way to the match.

I knew that the two Dundee grounds were on the same street, but I wasn't sure which one I would encounter first. I walked as far as I could up Fairbairn Street and then took a right and saw the other Dundee team's ground (Tannadice) in front of me. Typical, I thought, as I hurried on towards the floodlights further up the street, passing the Sky outside broadcast units advertising the Champions League – wishful thinking for the good folk of Dundee. Fortunately, I didn't have to go all the way round the ground to get to the away end as the Bob Shankly Stand was in front of me. I purchased my programme (£2.50) from the lad on the corner and headed towards the turnstile, parted with £15, got a receipt, visited the toilet and ventured out into the sunshine with seconds to spare for the 1.15 kick off – game on!

This was my first visit to Dens Park, home of the Dee, and my first impressions were mixed. The strangely shaped Main Stand and the mixture of terrace and waste ground opposite were at odds with the two new stands, one behind each goal.

The 'Well fans that I was in amongst were making plenty of noise. As I've said before, travelling supporters are essential if the game is to have a good atmosphere – and so should they perhaps be offered cheaper tickets?

With only three minutes gone, the Premier League visitors were ahead. From the off, the Steelmen looked slicker, fitter and were moving the ball around the bumpy looking pitch with ease. I later discovered that around 150 Dundee fans had worked through the night to get the pitch cleared of snow in a fantastic display of commitment and loyalty – Scottish football in the 21st century. The snow was piled up pitch-side and on the strange, barren knoll opposite the Main Stand – I wondered what used to be there.

Back to the football. Dundee were having a go at their esteemed visitors the crowd and the atmosphere had a big game feel about it.

No more goals before the break, and it was time to sample the local produce – 2-ish is a much better time to have a pie, I usually struggle to eat dinner after a 3.45 snack. Food and service were OK, usual choices. Two steak pies in two days are hard going. I could, however, drink Bovril till it was coming out of my ears.

I returned to the stand, planning to read the programme, which never happened as the half-time announcements grabbed my attention. The speaker gave an account of the club's precarious financial position and the huge efforts being made to raise money – more than £200,000 raised to date – with all and sundry doing their bit, even ex-Dundee United players. It would be a tragedy if this famous club went under, particularly for the fans (during the interval a song was played in the memory of one fan and you could really feel the strong community spirit).

I started thinking again about the issue of having two stadiums in one street. Surely the good people of Dundee, the council, local businesses and the football authorities could get round the table and give the city a new stadium to be proud of? Replacing the two with one shared stadium looks like a no-brainer to me. Why not redevelop one and turn the other into a training/leisure facility for the clubs and the local community? OK, easier said than done, but where there's a will there's a way.

Second half under way, and Motherwell scored almost immediately.

Ye Olde Dens Park

Stuart McCall was having a good day as the new 'Well manager and his team continued to press. Dundee hadn't given up though and they were unlucky on a couple of occasions. Both teams kept up the tempo to the end, with a few meaty challenges going in. The premier side were more clinical in their finishing and scored another two goals. Dundee's miserable afternoon got worse when Griffiths was sent off as the game reached its climax. The majority of the 4,285 crowd didn't have much to shout about but it had been an entertaining game and the 4-0 scoreline probably flattered the visitors a touch. The sun was going down behind the South Stand when the final whistle blew. Many of the Dee fans had already left and I headed out before the team came over to salute the fans. I passed the other stadium on my way back – how ridiculous this set-up is.

I was soon on the A90 and heading south. Poor Dundee, what if the 25-point deduction that they have appealed is enforced, I wondered, would they survive if they dropped to Division Two?

Scottish football needs a strong challenge from the Dundee clubs, preferably in the top division. I realise that amalgamation is out of the question, but could jointly addressing the stadium issue provide a platform for change and lead to a better future for the two clubs and the communities?

More questions than answers. I was also thinking about all the nonsense about going back to a ten-team top division – give us a break, please. There would be a place for Dundee in an extended top division, they are big enough and would enhance the league, but they need to get back on an even keel, the sooner the better.

The drive home was bearable as most of it was done in good light – one of the primary reasons I've come round to favouring early kick offs is safety. As I've said before, it's time to prioritise the wellbeing of the fans, rather than the requirements of the television channels.

Quote of the day – *Motherwell fans: 'There's only one Rab Douglas.'*
The big man had an off day.

GAME	DUNDEE VERSUS MOTHERWELL
DIVISION	SCR4
DATE	SUN 9 JAN 2011, KO 1.15PM
VENUE	DENS PARK, ATTENDANCE 4,285
SCORE	0-4

MATCH STATS:
HTTP://WWW.SCOTTISHFA.CO.UK/SCOTTISH_CUP_FIXTURE_DETAILS.
CFM?PAGE=1988&MATCHID=105282

21

THE WEE ROVERS V THE GABLE ENDIES

Junkyard Rovers

FOR A THIRD DIVISION clash at Cliftonhill, home of the 'famous' Albion Rovers, it was another awful day. Although it was blowing a gale and there was heavy rain on, the journey up the coast was OK and I got parked outside the ground 25 minutes ahead of the 3 o'clock start. *Off* and *On the Ball* had kept me entertained en route but the latter was starting to become boring. The constant talk of referees' mistakes, managers' indiscipline, players' contracts and the like has to stop. Entire radio shows are now devoted to everything but the beautiful game. The focus must move back to the football on the park… the passing, the skill, the commitment. Our friends in the media have a part to play in the resurrection of Scottish football.

And talking of resurrections, I think there's one due for the Rovers.

Passing this ground on many occasions over the years, I'd often wondered what the Rovers were like. I knew very little about the Albion, one of Scotland's oldest football clubs – now it was time to find out more.

There wasn't much activity as I approached the ground's red and yellow corrugated facade emblazoned with 'Reigart Demolition', which makes it look as if you are entering a scrapyard. I purchased my programme from the vendor at the turnstile and confused him somewhat when I enquired how much it was.

'One pound fifty,' he replied, 'everyone knows.'

I thanked him and moved on.

'Busy today?' I asked as I handed over my tenner at the turnstile.

'Got about nine in so far,' she replied, smiling.

What am I doing? I asked myself.

Everyone present seemed to be on first-name terms and they were all wishing one another a happy New Year. I followed the 'crowd'

Development potential?

(which actually included the proverbial one man and his dog), and headed up the stairs.

The Rovers were founded in 1882 and it certainly felt like I had travelled back in time – this had to be the worst stadium yet. 'Stadium' is probably the wrong word for the collection of old wooden and steel components surrounding a bumpy looking football pitch. Behind each goal there were grassy slopes and what looked like an old gravel running track surrounded the playing surface. I was still taking it all in when I noticed a silver Range Rover driving along behind the goals to my right and parking next to the Main Stand – now that's what I call a privileged parking space.

The snack bar, housed in a portacabin unit, was staffed by two friendly women. Incredibly, they had no steak pies, so I had to settle for a chicken and mushroom slice and a Bovril – a change is as good as a rest. The food was OK and the homely feel of its catering set-up reminded me of Alloa with its larger than usual selection – good on them.

Teams out and it's game on at Cliftonhill. Strangely, the managers and coaching staff were out on the pitch too. This was because the dugouts were opposite the Main Stand, something I don't remember having seen before. It was good to see the local boys clubs supplying the ball boys, although I don't know how delighted the boys would have felt at the privilege a wee while later when the rain started lashing down.

The game was a bit scrappy to start with but soon both teams were having a go (definitely more common in the lower divisions). Even so, the quality of football was pretty poor and this was having an impact on the mood in the stands. There was virtually no shouting or cheering, just moans and groans from the predominantly older spectators. A few youngsters in the terraced section occasionally burst into life, most notably after the visitors took the lead and probably in response to the handful of Montrose supporters who celebrated the goal. As the first half approached its conclusion, rain was pelting down and the old stand roof was rattling and whistling in the wind.

It was good to stand during the interval as the very small wooden seats were uncomfortable. I reckoned they must have been from around 1882 when people were much smaller, because no one there could sit properly for any length of time – most fans sat with their legs draped over the seat in front. This was not a problem as the stadium announcer confirmed that only 312 people were in the ground, and I honestly thought that was a bit on the generous side. I flicked through the programme and kept an eye on the rain battering against the window next to me. The floodlights were beaming down and I wondered how much they cost to run – a fortune, no doubt. The programme was quite interesting and kept me amused until the players re-emerged. Everything settled down again for the second half, except the weather.

Albion had a real go in the second half with Montrose mostly restricted to counter-attacking. A couple of the players were trying to dribble with the ball and although the outcomes were unsuccessful, it was good to see. Another interesting point about the lower leagues is the number of red and yellow cards issued – certainly in my experience, less than in the Premier League and First Division. It's nice to see the game played in a sporting manner.

The Rovers pressure was incessant but typically Montrose broke up the park and scored. I've seen this so many times already this season. The whistle signalled the end of the match and the stadium slowly emptied out into the dark, wet streets – time for home and the final scores on the radio.

A window of opportunity

Waiting for the classifieds on Radio Scotland, I needed one result for a double – that would be the icing on the cake. Strangely, I'd enjoyed my day. The football hadn't been great, nor was the stadium, but there was something about the whole experience. I'm probably just an old romantic at heart when it comes to Scottish football, but there's little time for sentiment and I worry for the future of the Albion. Who, apart from the couple of hundred diehards, would want to spend part of their afternoon at Cliftonhill Stadium? Where do the Rovers fit into the organogram of Scottish football? To me, there seem to be too many clubs just doing their own thing, primarily just to survive, and while I commend this, what is the point? Are they contributing to the upper echelons of the game in this country – the way it should be structured? Or are they just making up the numbers and doing something they've always done?

A few months later, a chance meeting at Luton Airport with Paul Martin, the Albion Rovers manager, gave me an invaluable insight into the Wee Rovers. In the bar with some work colleagues, the topic of conversation turned to football and I suddenly recognised the 'strange supporter' that had been sitting a few seats away from me at Galabank a few months previously. I say strange because he was sitting in amongst the Annan fans yet shouting instructions to the Albion players and getting a response – I would never have worked it out to this day that he was the manager. Anyway, I mentioned the review I was undertaking and we were soon in deep conversation. Some of his stories astounded me. All credit to the army of people, like Paul, who work tirelessly, many unpaid, for the game in this country. The passion, commitment and devotion you find in the lower reaches of

Scottish football gives me great hope for the future.

And the season turned out to be a good one for the Albion. Success in the nail-biting play-offs means a crack at Division Two. Great news for the club and the fans with different teams to watch and some new grounds to visit, but more pressure for the club to make ends meet. And the expectations of the fans will be higher – give us more success. Fortunately, with guys like Paul and his chairman, clubs like Albion will continue to play a part in Scottish football folklore. They've survived thus far and who knows what the future might bring.

Quote of the day – *Rovers fan 'We could end up going doon at this rate.' Can a Third Division team go down?*

GAME	ALBION ROVERS VERSUS MONTROSE
DIVISION	SFL3
DATE	SAT 15 JAN 2011, KO 3PM
VENUE	CLIFTONHILL STADIUM, ATTENDANCE 312
SCORE	0-2

MATCH STATS:
HTTP://WWW.SCOTTISHFOOTBALLLEAGUE.COM/FOOTBALL/THIRD/RESULTS/3284134/

22

THE WARRIORS V THE DIAMONDS

Artificially Beautiful

ANOTHER BITTER WINTER'S DAY. Today's preferences were East Fife or Stenhousemuir, two 'giants' of the Scottish game, both plying their trade in the Second Division. The decision was taken out of my hands when East Fife's game was called off due to the weather and I headed north for my first ever visit to Ochilview.

I had no idea where the stadium was, indeed I couldn't recall ever being in Stenhousemuir before so the old SatNav kept me right after exiting the M876. No problems getting parked, in the school on Rae Street, and I was soon heading past the toffee factory and onwards towards the home of the Warriors.

I was pleasantly surprised by the town which was much nicer than I had expected, and it has good links to the motorway network. However, one downside for Stenhousemuir FC is the close proximity of so many other senior clubs. This area is saturated with them and when you factor in the pull of the Old Firm, it's incredible that they've all survived this long.

Plenty going on en route to the stadium, lots of Airdrie fans as well, and I was looking forward to the game. The £11 I handed over to the turnstile attendant was quickly stuffed into a small cash box and I clicked through into the ground.

Numerous supporters were congregating in the area beyond the turnstiles, due to the snack bar and 'club shop' both being strategically positioned before you enter the all-seated Main Stand.

I decided to purchase my refreshments and joined the lengthy queue where I spotted an advertisement for Ladies Day Hospitality – now that's a great idea.

The service was excellent and I was soon at the front, studying the extensive menu. I was tempted by the home-made soup but stuck with the traditional steak pie and Bovril, good value and tasty.

The players were going through their warm-ups on the artificial surface and the place was filling up nicely. Game on!

And what a game it was.

Excellent from the start, two teams totally committed to playing a crisp, passing game, fast and furious end-to-end stuff with a good skill level. The games I've seen on artificial surfaces and in good weather stand out: long balls are few and far between and the players seem to focus on the passing game but still put in the tackles – something I was always wary of when playing on Astroturf, albeit that was 30 years ago. The technology has improved significantly, as has the players' confidence in it, therefore for Scotland these types of surfaces are a must.

Half time was soon upon us and it was still 0-0. It was cold so it was good to stand for a while. I read the 'programme' in about a minute and a half – easily the worst offering yet, a complete waste of money.

It was great to see so many families in the stadium. I noticed various sets of goalposts stored around the perimeter, which suggested that there were lots of other football-related things going on outwith match days – indeed, probably the only worthwhile aspect of the programme was that it advertised the youth development side of the club. Anyway, it was good to see that the stadium was getting used for more than just the senior games – another huge plus for the artificial surface.

Second half, floodlights on, and full throttle from the off. It's a pity the atmosphere in the stands didn't match the action on the pitch.

For a second week in a row the dugouts were across from the Main Stand. I think I prefer to hear the managers' rants though – it adds to the atmosphere. Incredibly, there were still piles of snow around the pitch weeks after the last snowfall. The action was relentless but in a con-

Stenhousemuir, Norway!

Classic stadium entrance

trolled manner and the Warriors had the upper hand. All credit to the Diamonds, they stuck to their game plan and played some great stuff. My enjoyment was abruptly ended by a call from my wife regarding a very ill elderly relative and I left what was arguably the best game of the season so far, with 15 minutes to go.

An hour later I was back home, disappointed that I had missed the home side's winner. However, I felt much more optimistic for Scottish football than I had on leaving Albion Rovers.

The Warriors seemed to have a close link with the local community, something that is not always the case. Ochilview Park left a lot to be desired, the toilets were awful and there didn't seem to be much in the way of facilities. However, the jewel in the crown was the pitch. The home fans seemed to be a decent bunch but they need to get behind their team a bit more.

A few players did catch my eye and probably could step up a division. The club might struggle though, simply because of the number of teams around them, all competing for a share of the disposable income and the precious personal time of the local supporters.

However, like many others, the club is now a Community Interest Company (CIC) and its website gives details of youth, community and academy links. The value of the pitch in terms of usage and generating revenue is also emphasised.

The Ladies Day Hospitality also intrigued me – with girls' and women's leagues now firmly established, why not have more events for... the Warriorettes?

Quote of the day – *Warriors fan: 'This is some f***ing game!'*

GAME   STENHOUSEMUIR VERSUS AIRDRIE UNITED

DIVISION   SFL2

DATE   SAT 22 JAN 2011, KO 3PM

VENUE   OCHILVIEW PARK, ATTENDANCE 819

SCORE   1-0

MATCH STATS:

HTTP://WWW.SCOTTISHFOOTBALLLEAGUE.COM/FOOTBALL/SECOND/
RESULTS/3284200/

23

THE TON V THE STAGGIES

Cappielower

THE USUAL SATURDAY morning routine was under way when news of some postponements captured my attention but the Ton's game was still on and by 2 o'clock I was in Greenock, parked and listening to the radio boys building up the passion.

As I watched the supporters on their way to the stadium, I imagined the once thriving shipyards and wondered what the atmosphere would have been like at Cappielow Park back then on match days, when it must have been a recreational hub for the masses from the yards. Despite the fact that Greenock has undergone quite a transformation in recent years, with new office blocks and flats dominating the coastline, the one thing apparently untouched by change is Cappielow Park. What an eyesore it is in the midst of all the redevelopment.

It's just not acceptable that so many Scottish football clubs ply their trade in dilapidated surroundings that haven't been upgraded for decades. These clubs have failed the fans – and they forget that the fans are the lifeblood of the game at their peril. Imagine any other type of leisure or recreation facility that failed to invest in the building that produces the majority of its revenue – would it still be in business? I doubt it. The people at the helm take the loyalty of fans for granted. They need to start paying respect to their needs and recognising that investment in the spectator experience is crucial for the future of the club.

OK, rant over and it's back to the fitba'. This was my first visit to Cappielow and I was looking forward to it. As a former Glasgow shipyard worker myself, I had worked with many people from this area and remembered their passion for the club. Indeed, I remember a pre-Souness Smith era victory for the Ton over Glasgow Rangers being rowdily celebrated in a Govan Shipyard by the boys from the

Where's the seats? Where's the roof?

'tail o the bank'. Things have changed though. Morton are now in the bottom half of the First Division and it's been a while since they played in the Premier League.

With about 20 minutes to kick off, I headed towards the floodlights and the big crane that dominates the skyline. I was a touch miffed to discover that there was a car park directly opposite the ground and consoled myself with the fact that I was £3 better off and wouldn't get stuck in the inevitable traffic jam at the end of the game (actually the police and wardens ensured a constant flow from the car park and I won't be making the same mistake next time). I carried on up towards the railway bridge, looking for the main entrance. If I'd been expecting an elegant doorway engineered by the finest the Clyde had to offer, I'd have been disappointed. At the turnstile I handed over £17, which was a touch expense for a First Division fixture. There was a reasonable enough 'parent and child' deal at £20; I did wonder how much additional kids would be. After taking some photographs, I purchased my usual pie and Bovril from a predictable menu, climbed the stairs and ventured out into the winter sunshine.

Grim as Cappielow Park looks from the outside, it's not all that bad inside. The open terrace to my right was a real throwback to a bygone era, although I don't know how appealing it would be when the weather was less favourable. Straight across from me was a covered terrace and to the left, an uncovered seated area. A mixed bag, but pleasant enough.

The club mascot and cheerleaders were doing their thing on the pitch and the tannoy was blaring out music and club announcements. Game on at Cappielow! It was end-to-end stuff during the opening stages, though not a lot of quality on show, and Morton started to take control amid a few shouts from the home crowd. The atmosphere was virtually non-existent until Ross County scored against the run of play and loud cheers erupted from the other end of the Main Stand, where the visiting fans all the way from Dingwall were celebrating the goal – excellent. The end-to-end stuff continued, mostly route one. When the ref blew for half time the visitors were one up, much to the annoyance of the somewhat elderly local crowd.

During the break I read the £2 programme from cover to cover and made a foray downstairs, where it was quite busy, the home supporters chatting convivially making the sort of community atmosphere that's a definite plus point for the smaller clubs. A few cheers from above signalled that the players were out again and everyone made their way back to the floodlit arena.

The second half was almost a carbon copy of the first – then Morton scored a very good goal. It was just as well they scored when they did as the fans were really starting to get on the players' backs. Morton eventually doubled their tally and held on till the end. A good result for the home side. As I left I noticed that the grass pitch seemed to have held out well.

Snarled up in heavy traffic in Greenock, I had plenty time to mull over the advantages of earlier kick offs (less traffic) and the potential for Morton in adopting the combined football and athletic (or similar) club format that used to be more prevalent. This strikes me as being a sensible way to better utilise the facilities – so many stadiums are white elephants for most of the time. At Cappielow this would definitely mean a new artificial playing surface for all-weather usage. As at Airdrie and Stenhousemuir, I'm sure it would be a worthwhile investment.

The crowd on the day was 1,675, a bit disappointing for a town the size of Greenock (population around 45,000). Probably the most disappointing aspect was that the football club seemed to be stuck in a time warp in the midst of so much urban renewal and this is surprising because they were the first football club in Scotland to form a supporters trust. I know that events forced their hand to an extent

due to administration, but it would have been good if the supporters'
vision for the Ton had included a modern facility to match their
surroundings. Hopefully it's on their agenda.

Quote of the day – *The song 'Night boat to Cairo' – apt with Egypt in
turmoil.*

GAME	GREENOCK MORTON VERSUS ROSS COUNTY
DIVISION	SFL1
DATE	SAT 29 JAN 2011, KO 3PM
VENUE	CAPPIELOW PARK, ATTENDANCE 1,675
SCORE	2-1

MATCH STATS:
HTTP://WWW.SCOTTISHFOOTBALLLEAGUE.COM/FOOTBALL/FIRST/
RESULTS/3284243/

24

THE ARABS V THE HIBEES

Tangerine Dreams

THE TWO-GAME WEEKEND was taking its toll. I procrastinated for about an hour before eventually getting organised for my second trip to the City of Discovery in a month. On my previous visit the weather meant I never managed to get a good look round Dens Park and I wanted more photographs, which I took on my way to Tannadice – I still can't get my head round having two stadiums in the same street.

Today's kick-off time – 1.15 – was by now a firm favourite of mine. I wandered around watching the fans, most of whom were draped in black and tangerine, as were the stewards and the stadium – the sea of orange reminded me of the Dutch national team and fans.

The place was busy but calm, and this no doubt suited the many families that were making their way to the game. I joined a small queue at one of the turnstiles in the George Fox Stand. Eventually I got to the front and handed over my £22. The guy behind the partition seemed flustered – that was the reason for the slow throughput, the other being the prehistoric monetary system in operation, involving tupperware tubs full of notes and piles of change.

In the busy foyer I got my bearings and checked out the shop, where I found the old programmes and other memorabilia on display very interesting.

Next on the agenda was the snack bar, after which I retreated to a perimeter shelf to consume the usual fare. The quality of pie on offer at Tannadice was fine, but I was sick of them. No more from now on – crisps and chocolate would suffice.

Kick-off time fast approaching, I followed the steady flow out into the cold, orange light of the arena. I made my way down the steps looking for a seat that wasn't reserved and settled on one halfway down where I was surrounded by season ticket holders, all of whom

Floodlights blazing early afternoon?

knew each other and were probably wondering who the guy in the black hat was.

The area I had chosen was filling up nicely and the story was similar in the stand to my left. It was virtually empty directly opposite, by the dugouts, as was the other small stand to my right. The stadium was much smaller than it looked on TV and was a real mix of structures and shapes; the only consistent aspect was the 'orangeness'. As the teams emerged there were a few cheers (and that was about it in terms of atmosphere until the third United goal) and the game got under way.

The football was faster and slicker compared to the offering in Greenock – but it was still lacking in quality, probably due to the speed of play. The high tempo was producing end-to-end football, much of which was route one. High balls were the order of the day even when things slowed a touch, the big centre forwards being the focal point of most of the attacks. United scored, deservedly, and Hibs seemed to sense yet another defeat, though they never threw in the towel – and maybe that's one of their problems, still trying to play football rather than shutting up shop and becoming hard to beat.

The half-time whistle blew and gradually the stadium rose. It was good to stand and I enjoyed the break, primarily because I felt a bit warmer, and also thanks to the entertainment. The pitch was immediately invaded by youngsters bringing with them all the apparatus required to play football. It was great to see young local kids playing on the 'big pitch' at the 'tip of the football iceberg' in the local area – what a motivator that might turn out to be. I watched the

United in nostalgia

youngsters while flicking through the programme, which was full of good stuff.

Second half under way and another two goals rounded off a good performance for the home side. Another defeat for the struggling Hibees. I've seen enough of them this season to confidently predict that they will survive in the top flight and I hope they do, we need a strong Hibernian. And United, they've struggled to reach the levels that culminated in a Scottish Cup victory last season. However, as usual they do seem to have a conveyor belt of young talent coming through and should be OK.

Game over and it was easy enough to get out of the stadium. There had been a pretty poor crowd of just over 6,000. Why such a paltry attendance? Dundee is Scotland's fourth biggest city (population approx. 150,000), so surely we should expect more supporters at the city's premier club? Similarly, I'm struggling to understand just why the 'second tier' clubs Hearts, Hibs, Dundee United and Aberdeen have such low average attendances compared to the Old Firm. What is the attraction with Celtic and Rangers that the others can't match? Would attendances improve if the big two moved to another league? I honestly don't know. Would reconstruction of the leagues improve attendances? Yes, in my view a bit more variety would whet the appetite.

All the way home I thought about how the clubs could move forward and prosper and I kept coming back to the fact that football is archetypal; 3 o'clock Saturday kick offs, pies and Bovril, poor facilities, winter… Drastic change is required to get more fans through the turnstiles – this is the crux of the matter.

Two hours later and I was in the gym in Troon pounding on the running machine. I thought more about the Arabs and how inefficient the set-up and stadium seemed. The cost of staging a game must be considerable, particularly in an old stadium. The two Dundee clubs must get their heads together – it would be beneficial and could even save Dundee. Imagination and courage will be required, two qualities desperately needed to pull Scottish football out of the doldrums.

Quote of the day – *Very polite United fan: 'Jolly good show.'*

GAME	DUNDEE UNITED VERSUS HIBERNIAN
DIVISION	SPL
DATE	SUN 30 JAN 2011, KO 1.15PM
VENUE	TANNADICE PARK, ATTENDANCE 6,215
SCORE	3-0

MATCH STATS:
HTTP://WWW.SCOTPREM.COM/CONTENT/DEFAULT.ASP?PAGE=S10_1_1
&WORKINGDATE=2011-1-30

25

THE BAIRNS V THE TON

Parking Penalties

FALKIRK STADIUM WAS my venue for Game 25. Twenty minutes before kick off, I handed over £4 to park on a bit of waste ground adjacent to the away end of the superb new stadium (valet parking in the USA is cheaper). The Main Stand in particular looked very good, it reminded me of Hampden. Generally, there was a good buzz about the place and although its immediate vicinity is barren, it does mean plenty of parking spaces and quick, hassle free access and exit.

Programme purchased, I headed for the Main Stand turnstiles and approached one of the hi-viz brigade for advice on entry. He informed me that there was no pay-in gate at this section and I should go to the other end of the stand. This meant I would be at the opposite end of the ground from where I'd parked so I quickly decided to go and sit among the Morton fans. Surprisingly, there were no prices displayed above the entrance to the away stand and I enquired about the cost: '£15.50' was the reply, the electronic display changed to green and I was in the spacious foyer and making the customary visit to the snack bar. Now I know I said I wouldn't eat another pie, but that was two weeks ago (last week's game at St Johnstone was called off). Anyway, I was peckish, so, steak pie and Bovril it was, from the usual limited menu.

The place was filling up nicely as I took my seat high up in the stand. To my left was the open section (I'm assuming the plan is to complete this stand one day), to my right was the Main Stand, and straight ahead, behind the other set of goals, more home supporters. The PA was absolutely blaring and the cheerleaders were out in force. Pity the supporters weren't making much noise, or maybe they couldn't be heard over the din.

Both teams started slowly and got slower. There were lots of high

The imposing Falkirk Stadium

balls, misplaced passes and mistimed challenges (none of them sinister), a very poor showing. With the fans so very quiet, I recalled that the old ground, Brockville, was infamous for its raucous atmosphere.

The high balls and poor quality finishing continued unabated, as did the steady stream of Morton fans entering the stand late. I wondered what proportion of fans watched the entire 90 minutes. I felt relieved when the first half eventually petered out. I had spent much of it checking scores on the iPhone and staring out over the waste ground. This was not exactly turning out to be good value for money (approximately £40 including fuel). The ref signalled for the break. Time for a read.

The Bairns' programme contained plenty of interesting information on the club, youth set-ups, former players and games – there was some excellent historical stuff. Looking back at teams from yesteryear always jogs the memory and I was lost in thought when the Ton came running back out for the second half.

It turned out to be the proverbial game of two halves with the second half much better all round, primarily because the ball was on the deck. The Bairns started to dominate and looked the most likely to score, however Morton caught them out on a couple of occasions and could have scored if only the finishing had been better. The game charged on under the floodlights. Grey sky had replaced the sunshine

There's a big gap to the left!

and the temperature was dropping. The opposite was happening on the pitch. Tempers were flaring and all of a sudden Morton were down to nine men. Inevitably, Falkirk scored. It had been coming even before the sending-offs and I couldn't see any way back for Morton. Suddenly things changed again when the Bairns had a player dismissed. Three off in the one game – I couldn't quite get my head around this one as it hadn't been a dirty game at all. The Ton tried in vain for an equaliser but it wasn't to be. Falkirk held on and gained a valuable three points for their promotion quest.

I was out of the car park and heading towards the M9 in no time. This got me thinking about the out-of-town stadium versus the town-centre stadium – which is best? In an ideal world, I would prefer a town centre location with good public transport links, parking, and other sports and leisure facilities nearby. However, on the tour so far, stadiums have either been in populated town areas or in new, out-of-town developments. There are arguments for and against both and in reality it's horses for courses: what the clubs have they've got to make the best of. For future developments though, I think they need to weigh up the options.

Back home I was soon sitting down to steak and chips and thinking about my day. I was optimistic for Falkirk, they seemed to be going in the right direction. This impression was mainly down to the stadium, a far more appealing venue than many I've visited. On balance, I was tending to favour new developments. Odds-on they are more cost-efficient to run as well. Clubs that expect supporters to come along to dilapidated grounds are not only treating fans with disrespect, they have to wake up to the fact that getting the infrastructure right is fundamental to their survival.

Quote of the day – Morton fan: 'Some draught comes in that big gap!' (Referring to where the fourth stand should be.)

GAME	FALKIRK VERSUS GREENOCK MORTON
DIVISION	SFL1
DATE	SAT 12 FEB 2011, KO 3PM
VENUE	FALKIRK STADIUM, ATTENDANCE 3,636
SCORE	1-0

MATCH STATS:
HTTP://WWW.SCOTTISHFOOTBALLLEAGUE.COM/FOOTBALL/FIRST/
RESULTS/3284412/

26

THE GALABANKIES V THE WEE ROVERS

A Gala Day in Annan for the Albion

ARBROATH AND FORFAR were on the radar until the weather again intervened and a quick rethink highlighted the Third Division clash in the southwest – Galabank Stadium it was.

The journey was easier than expected with no weather problems or other delays and I was parked on waste ground behind the away end just after 2.30. With plenty of time until kick off, I lingered in the car listening to a discussion on Radio Scotland about the return of various veterans to the Scottish game, most notably Neil McCann at Dundee and Charlie Miller at Clyde. Great stuff, that's what I had been expecting in the lower leagues.

The car park was a few seconds' walk from the entrance to the north end (that's something I really enjoy about the smaller clubs – access/ egress parking etc is so much easier). I took some photographs before heading round to the main entrance, adjacent to which is the social club. I purchased my programme and was briefly considered going in for a drink. The flexibility of the car has its downsides, alcohol being one, and I decided to head back round to the away end – far from the temptation of the bevvy.

The walk back down the road was very enjoyable. The stadium PA was blasting out 'All Night Long' (Rainbow) and it could be heard for miles. I bounced back to the turnstile next to the artificial training pitches, parted with my £9 (great price) and walked into Galabank for the first time. A member of the hi-viz brigade was consulted regarding toilets and snack bar and first stop was the portacabin loo (no hot water), then on to the 'garden hut' snack bar where I ordered crisps, Bovril and a Marathon (the latter much to the bewilderment of the young chap who was serving). After realising my mistake, I eventually got my Snickers bar and headed towards the all-seated Main Stand.

The gates of Annan

I had no idea how much each individual item cost, there was no price list or menu.

I took a seat next to the demarcation chain at the back of the stand. Surrounded by about 25 Albion fans, I felt they all knew there was an interloper in their midst. The stand was the only seated section, the other three being terraced, and it was easily the busiest. The social club end was the focus of pre-match activity both in a footballing sense and for the fans. Kick-off time was fast approaching and the Rovers fans were cranking up the noise.

What a game it turned out to be. The start was pretty even, both teams trying to play football on a bumpy pitch. I was reminded of the amateur games my dad used to take me to when I was a boy. The players, too, looked strangely familiar, archetypal Charlie Adam but definitely not as good. A steward intervened when one of the fans started swearing loudly – quite right, there was no need for the verbal nonsense that he was inflicting on the entire stadium. The visitors played some excellent football and it was surprising that they were only one up at half time as they had created a multitude of chances. The Rovers fans were clearly bewildered by the low score line.

It took about two minutes to read the programme cover to cover.

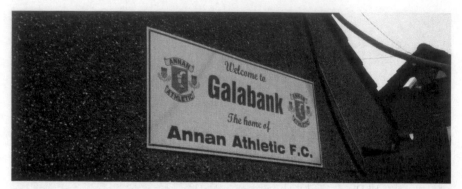

A Gala welcome

Gazing around the small stadium I asked myself, is this really senior football in Scotland? I thought back to Albion's rusting Main Stand, which was huge in comparison. This was definitely more like a junior outfit. As with the Rovers, where do they fit into the structure of Scottish football? Are the two clubs feeding the bigger organisations – should they be? As usual, more questions than answers. I do get the feeling that some clubs are just making up the numbers – they seem to lack direction and purpose. I could be wrong and would willingly stand corrected. The blaring music snapped me out of deep thought and it was time to check the scores on the iPhone – nothing like a punt on the football on a Saturday.

Teams back out and at it hell for leather from the off. It was much colder but the action on the park was truly warming up, challenges flying in, then two goals from the home side and the rowdy bespectacled Rovers followers were finally silenced. All of a sudden the home crowd raised their voices and started getting behind their team. Then another twist, as an Annan player got his marching orders. After that, Albion really went for it. Incredibly, the visitors scored in injury time to level things. What an excellent game – entertaining throughout, four goals and a sending-off.

Within minutes of the final whistle I was on the road home.

For Annan Athletic, another Third Division club struggling to make ends meet, what could turn things round for them? Young local talent is arguably the one thing that would make a difference. OK, everyone will say 'more money', but that's only a short-term fix. Local lads playing for the team and then progressing is the way forward. Money would help but it's not the be all and end all.

I was interested to learn more about the local set-ups and where the club sits within those structures. Further research revealed that they are part of the Dumfries and Galloway Youth Football Development Association (DGYFDA) which promotes football in a structured way. This investment in youth should pay dividends long term, both for the club and the community in general.

Two hours later, I was home. The journey had been OK, there had been just enough light to keep the eyes from getting strained. I had enjoyed my day and I'm sure most of the crowd had too. My visit to Galabank had been interesting but I had niggling doubts as to whether they belonged in the senior levels of Scottish football. I think there are too many clubs in the four divisions – much more debate will be required on this one.

Quote of the day – Albion fan: 'Let's take a point from this dump.' Has Cliftonhill been rebuilt?

GAME   ANNAN ATHLETIC VERSUS ALBION ROVERS
DIVISION   SFL3
DATE   SAT 19 FEB 2011, KO 3PM
VENUE   GALABANK STADIUM, ATTENDANCE 467
SCORE   2 2

MATCH STATS:
HTTP://WWW.SCOTTISHFOOTBALLLEAGUE.COM/FOOTBALL/THIRD/
RESULTS/3284478/

27

THE SONS V THE BLUE TOON

Midweek Madness

WHAT WOULD DUMBARTON bring to the party? I decided to find out on a cold February night after staying on at work in Paisley office and then heading west with darkness descending and dampness in the air. On a night like this, home was the sensible option but I was determined to keep to my schedule.

Dumbarton Rock completely dominates the skyline and in relation to it the Strathclyde Homes Stadium looks tiny. I was over an hour early and briefly considered taking a walk around the ground. The weather and the gloom curtailed my enthusiasm for a wander. The decision was to get the laptop out and finish writing up Saturday's review. From Annan to Dumbarton – not exactly the crème de la crème, but real fitba', what it's all about.

I clocked that most of the drivers arriving were wearing the Sons tracksuits. I must have parked illegally in the players/officials car park (adjacent to the front door of the stadium), but the expected knock on the window never materialised so I continued with my account of my visit to Galabank Stadium, half-listening to the nonsense that Radio Clyde spouts every night – only one of the many commercial stations that perpetrate a constant flow of rubbish. For me this is one of Scottish football's major problems – and unfortunately, one that's unlikely to go away.

The in-depth analysis of every referee's decision, manager's comment and anything else that gets a reaction from fans is pointless. What we need is a football show that concentrates on football; the nice touches, great goals, younger players coming through and games to look forward to. Stations in the west of the country are particularly monotonous because of the underlying sectarian issues – we really need to give it a rest.

At 7.15, outside the bright facade of the main entrance, I enquired about cash gates and programmes. The friendly stewardess pointed me in the right direction and I wandered off past the supporters' social club/bar (I'll need to do a review without the car), and round to the cash turnstile where I handed over £12 and entered the spacious, modern foyer. The place was busy – a door from the social club led directly into the stadium, easy access for beer. I purchased the 'two in one' programme and at the snack bar where I submitted to the usual steak pie and Bovril. Service was swift, prices average (£3.25), the menu limited. Evening meal devoured, I took some photographs and strolled out into the arena.

I chose a seat towards the rear of the Main Stand – well, there is only one stand – and settled down for the match. This was my first visit to the stadium and also the first time I'd seen either of the two teams in the flesh. After this survey I will definitely continue going to see more different teams, that aspect has been most enjoyable.

Teams out, floodlights on and 'The Sons are the Ones' bellowing out from the PA. Both teams started at a high tempo with the Sons eventually getting the upper hand. The football was mostly played on the deck and a good move led to the home side's well-deserved first goal. Then a moment of madness changed the game. Peterhead had a man sent off just before half time which effectively ended their challenge.

I spent the break reading the double-issue programme which covered Saturday's match with Airdrie as well as tonight's encounter. Not much to write home about in terms of content, so I checked the

A dark night at the Rock

evening's investments on the iPhone. The fog looked to be coming down and I thought about the journey that the Peterhead players and fans (who were conspicuous by their silence) had in front of them. Midweek fixtures must be a real struggle for the teams located furthest north and south and their travelling fans, unless they are playing local rivals. I can really understand the thinking behind regional leagues. I wonder how many away fans travel to Peterhead for a midweek fixture – no doubt very few.

Peterhead rallied in the early stages of the second half but Dumbarton regained control, scored a couple of good goals and ran out comfortable winners. The football was good throughout and all credit to Peterhead, they never threw in the towel. The Sons' fans cheered every pass and clearly enjoyed their evening. The best games I've seen for this review have been in the Second Division and tonight's match was again to a good standard with both teams competing and, most importantly, trying to play football.

And the future for Dumbarton? I thought back to the programme supplement which advertised the 'Save the Sons for a Tenner' campaign. Difficult times indeed.

There is, however, change in the air across the board in Scottish football, and the fans will be the primary drivers. The Sons trust was one of the first supporter-led organisations to get a controlling interest in their club and like many others they are keen to have a say in the running of the organisation. The next step must be the governing bodies – the fans must have a say in them as well.

Quote of the day – *Dumbarton fan: 'Get it right up ye, if there's any of ye here.' (Aimed at any Peterhead fans that might have been in the stadium.)*

GAME	DUMBARTON VERSUS PETERHEAD
DIVISION	SFL2
DATE	TUES 22 FEB 2011, KO 7.30PM
VENUE	STRATHCLYDE HOMES STADIUM, ATTENDANCE 376
SCORE	3-0

MATCH STATS:
HTTP://WWW.SCOTTISHFOOTBALLLEAGUE.COM/FOOTBALL/SECOND/RESULTS/3365200/

28

THE LOONS V THE SONS

Sons Miss the Connection at Station Park

BEFORE I HAD TIME to draw breath, Game 28 was on the agenda. I ruled out Ross County and Elgin because both entailed an overnight stay. Montrose and East Fife were possibilities but I decided on Forfar, quite simply because it looked like being the best game and I had enjoyed the Sons' midweek performance. So Angus it was.

After various delays due to road works I finally arrived in Forfar at 2.45 and typically took a wrong turning. After a U-turn and some cheeky manoeuvres I was parked on Carseview Road just a few hundred yards from Station Park (there is no station in Forfar any more, it was axed in the Beeching cuts). Due to time constraints, I was unable to do my usual circuit of the ground and that was a pity as it was such a glorious setting, rolling fields and hills as the backdrop – peace and tranquillity.

It cost a very reasonable £11 to get in at the single turnstile. I found myself corralled in a restricted area with toilets and a snack bar to my left and stairs up into the Main Stand straight ahead. I purchased my lunch, £2.30 for a Forfar bridie and a small Bovril. It was a lovely, sunny day, a few degrees warmer than it has been recently. What a difference that makes. The teams were already out for the game so I chose a bench close to the stairs in the Main Stand.

Both teams went at it from the off with Dumbarton probably edging the first few minutes and it was therefore a bit surprising when the Loons took the lead with an excellent goal after five minutes. Most of the noise that followed the goal was generated by fans in the terraces. I was definitely in the posh seats where things were quieter and the clientele was on the older side.

Everyone seemed to be enjoying the sniff of spring in the air and I liked the stadium, there was a homely feel to it, unlike, for example,

The toilets were separate!

the Strathclyde Homes Stadium where the visitors ply their trade. I finished my bridie (not that impressed) while the game continued at a good tempo, both sides trying to play the passing game on what looked quite a lumpy pitch.

Dumbarton were rewarded for their efforts with a very good goal ten minutes before half time. This excellent free kick settled the score and the whistle signalled the end of a very entertaining first half. My attention turned to the programme and the stadium itself. The place was covered in advertising boards displaying the services of local businesses (indicating a good marketing department).

The summerhouse style snack bar did a roaring trade until a shower had everyone diving for cover. The programme was a quick read, so I turned my attention to my iPhone for the half-time results – the coupon was looking good again. Teams back out and again Dumbarton were really trying hard to win the game. The visitors were doing most of the entertaining, with the Loons restricted to the odd counter-attack. A number of good chances were missed, and typically, the team who had sat back and soaked up the pressure took the lead. Station Park was bouncing. The action continued to the final whistle with the battle on the park keeping everyone on the terraces warm as the temperature dropped – never get carried away by a few rays of sunshine when it's still winter.

Another stadium visited and more food for thought on the state of the beautiful game in Scotland. Forfar is the type of club that should be thriving – with the right approach and joined-up thinking, that is. And how joined up is this? The Loons and local neighbours Farmington Football Club have got together and applied for a new 3/4G synthetic pitch for Station Park.

Chairman Neill Wilson told the *Forfar Dispatch*, 'This is a unique, pivotal moment for the town of Forfar; it is our opportunity to step forward and say we want our senior football club to lead the way, to be an example of how a club can be the centre of the community, leading and not being led or, even worse, not involved at all. We want community involvement in the "Station Park Experience" where opportunities will exist for all sections of the community to receive benefit from this project.'

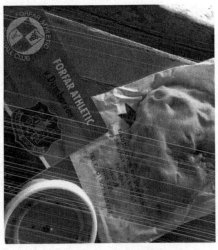

Athletic after a Forfar bridie?

The article expanded on how the all year/all weather use of the pitch would not only be for football matches and training but also for various other sports, with Station Park becoming a 'hub' for other activities such as school use and sports tournaments, and attracting a wide range of visitors. Is Scottish football finally awakening from its long slumber?

Quote of the day – *Forfar fan: 'Jesus Christ, Jesus Christ' every few seconds – maybe I missed something?*

GAME	FORFAR ATHLETIC VERSUS DUMBARTON
DIVISION	SFL2
DATE	SAT 26 FEB 2011, KO 3PM
VENUE	STATION PARK, ATTENDANCE 487
SCORE	2-1

MATCH STATS:
HTTP://WWW.SCOTTISHFOOTBALLLEAGUE.COM/FOOTBALL/SECOND/
RESULTS/3284554/

29

THE SHIRE V THE GABLE ENDIE

Shire Cuckoos Clocked at Ochilview

WITH MY OPTIONS limited due to an evening wedding reception I was set to attend, I took a look at the East Stirlingshire website. The Shire departed their own ground a few years ago and my destination was again Ochilview. En route I listened to the usual grumblings of Stuart and Tam on *Off the Ball*. The hilarity was followed by *On the Ball* where the fallout from Wednesday's Old Firm shame game continued unabated, Rangers manager Walter Smith saying he was weary of the fixture. Many fans, myself included, felt the same.

So there you have it – incredible media attention for all the wrong reasons. Hardly a mention of the football (not that it was a classic by any means), all the talk, as ever, concentrating on the behaviour of the players and coaching staff. It's my view that everyone – players, managers, supporters and the press pack – all have to take responsibility. If trouble on and off the terraces has the power to dominate media coverage, not only football, but society at large will suffer. The pernicious effect can't be overestimated.

On my arrival at Ochilview I took some photographs of the Montrose team bus, parted with £11 for a ticket and bought a programme from the turnstile attendant (that was handy). Absolutely scunnered by an excess of steak pies over the past weeks, I'd brought a sandwich, so my purchases at the snack bar were limited to Bovril, crisps and a caramel log.

Tammy Wynette was playing over the PA and the announcer took great delight in referring to the stadium as 'Lesser Firs Park' – tongue no doubt firmly in cheek. The place was filling up nicely although it wasn't as busy as the last time I was here.

Both teams started at a reasonable pace and the game was generally played on the deck, although there was definitely a significant difference

Which goals are we using?

in quality compared to the last visit's Second Division clash between Stenhousemuir and Airdrie. The 'home' side took the lead, much to the delight of their vociferous fans (best patter yet – aided and abetted by the Montrose goalie who appeared to have tights on). The game ebbed and flowed with neither team dominating. I thought the Shire Boys look very old-fashioned in their hooped strip. Some of the players were slightly built and looked very young – too young in fact, which concerned me a touch. Everyone was getting stuck in though, and the game was entertaining. Montrose missed a sitter and a controversial penalty claim by the Shire Boys was turned down. The ref's whistle brought relief from the sound of a heid-bursting horn blown by some balloon throughout the first period.

The £1.50 programme was an interesting read and I spent most of the break going through it and checking the half-time results on the iPhone – not particularly good news on the coupon front. There were lots of family groups among the Shire fans, who were all talking and laughing amongst themselves. But I should think that on some level they must have felt like cuckoos in someone else's nest and wondered whether they would ever get a ground of their own again.

Lost in my daydream, I actually missed the equaliser a few seconds into the second half. The few travelling Montrose supporters certainly enjoyed the moment and the 'home' fans were getting more concerned by the second. Another denied penalty claim further raised the temperature – which was welcome, because the pleasant spring day had reverted to winter. The visitors gradually took control of the game, much to the annoyance of the Shire fans. The excellent banter was replaced by the usual guttural verbal diarrhoea, all in front of all the kids as well – totally unnecessary. Then the inevitable happened: Montrose scored, deservedly, and the 'home' fans groaned in unison. The noise levels dropped considerably, as did my hopes of the coupon compensating me for some of the day's expenses.

On the drive home, I turned over the Shire's predicament in my mind. Generally I support the shared stadium principle where feasible, the Dundee 'no-brainer' being the prime example of serious benefits potentially to be reaped. But at this match there was nothing whatsoever for the ground-sharing club to attach themselves to and this alerted me to an important requirement: if clubs are going to share facilities, they need to be able to put their own brand or mark on them, even if it's just temporary – this is needed to help to strengthen the fan base.

Albeit Firs Park and 'lesser Firs Park' are (were) less than three miles away, the local aspect is somewhat lost. However, if ground sharing means the survival of a club then all opportunities much be explored and clubs and supporters must understand that this might be the way to go. Given that this area is saturated with senior clubs, restructuring may be the only option. Bit like my coupon – too many teams on it.

Quote of the day – *Shire fan: 'He's that stupid he would put a top hat on upside doon.'*

GAME	EAST STIRLINGSHIRE VERSUS MONTROSE
DIVISION	SFL3
DATE	SAT 5 MAR 2011, KO 3PM
VENUE	OCHILVIEW PARK, ATTENDANCE 306
SCORE	1-2

MATCH STATS:
HTTP://WWW.SCOTTISHFOOTBALLLEAGUE.COM/FOOTBALL/THIRD/
RESULTS/3284626/

30

THE GERS V KILLIE

Bear Necessities at Quiet Ibrox

DESTINATION IBROX. DUE to a planned night out in Edinburgh, Saturday games were off the agenda and the Sunday offering was the easiest, albeit not the preferred, option. Arbroath and Montrose had been on the radar, but Ibrox was definitely a good decision as more snowfalls had caused disruption on the roads and throughout the football cards – need I say more.

A visit to Ibrox was pencilled in as a midweek 'catch up' fixture. My schedule was tight and I wanted to keep the Premier League till the end and go midweek to 'local' games. It wasn't to be, however, and another opportunity for a weekend trip to a more distant venue had been lost. That left eight Saturdays/weekends to go, with 14 grounds still to visit – it was going to be a struggle. Anyway, back to today's offering.

I was parked by 2 o'clock and walked briskly towards the ticket office to the rear of the Govan Stand. As I photographed the stadium, it occurred to me that I have never done this before at the ground which is my 'spiritual home', a place I've been coming to for about 40 years. That got me thinking. Was there anywhere else that I'd been going to, regularly, for that length of time? No.

OK, the review was my purpose for being here and I would try and be impartial throughout – which might prove impossible for a lifelong Gers fan. I carried on towards the portacabins, enjoying the feel of being at a big game again; police horses, flag vendors, cars parked everywhere and, most importantly, a big crowd. I later checked back on the spreadsheet for an attendance similar to today's and was surprised to find that it was at Hampden the previous October, for Scotland against the reigning world champions, Spain. The Old Firm are right up there when it comes to packing them in every week. In UK

Flag day

terms, only Manchester United and Arsenal are in front.

As I approached the ticket office, I got a shout from a work colleague and chatted for a few minutes (this would happen on a number of occasions – it was good to be back) before heading for the ticket office. There was plenty going on around the place but thankfully the queue was easily contained within the building and I soon had my brief and was walking around the rear of the Govan, past Bar 72 and the Megastore.

At the corner of the Copland and Main stands, I met up with a friend and we discussed the Gers, Scottish football and life in general for almost an hour, before heading into our seats for the afternoon's entertainment. That's one thing I have missed, going to so many unfamiliar grounds – the social aspect. I did think about involving a few friends in the review but on second thoughts I decided to go it alone.

I made my way to the front section of the Broomloan Road Stand and handed over the £23 ticket that I'd purchased earlier. It was surprisingly empty at five to three and there was no last minute rush. I had to cast my mind back to the early '80s to remember a similar scenario at the home of the Gers – definitely a worrying sight. The rest of the ground was almost full though, and the average attendance remains around the 45,000 mark. It did peak at nearly 50,000 at the turn of the century but the global downturn has definitely had an effect. The teams came out and did the usual line-up and handshaking rituals, swapped ends. Kilmarnock had impressed me on the two previous occasions that I'd seen them this season so I was looking forward to the match even though both sides had a few big players missing.

The game was reasonably even in the opening period with the Gers getting a grip and dominating for the majority of the half. There wasn't much of an atmosphere inside the ground, even with the 'in house' band belting out their tunes, and to be honest the football wasn't exactly thrilling either. The cold was starting to bite (Scotland in the middle of March), and I was pleased when Rangers scored just before half time. The stadium rose in applause and the old blood got circulating again. At the whistle I made my way down into the bowels of the stand for a heat. No pie or Bovril, had enough of them for this season, but I did check out the menu – usual rubbish. I hung about for a few minutes, watching the adverts on the big TV screens, before heading back out into what is definitely one of the best sporting arenas that I have ever visited.

I flicked through the programme (only £2.50 these days) and watched the comings and goings of the Rangers faithful. There were more families around the place than I had ever noticed before, and they all seemed to be munching on fast food. It's not surprising that the stadium catering company, Azure, are so keen on lengthy contracts, having recently signed a deal for nine years, worth tens of millions of pounds.

The floodlights were on, the pitch looked good, the PA was blasting out birthday greetings and the like. In fact, the place was actually much livelier than it had been during play.

The teams ran back out and normal service was quickly resumed. Rangers continued where they left off, restricting Kilmarnock to the odd breakaway. Then the game was suddenly turned on its head when Kilmarnock were awarded, and scored, a 'soft' penalty. All of sudden tackles were flying in, the crowd were on their feet and the players were cheating at every opportunity – why is this so prevalent in the top league? I focused on the players for a moment. They looked like footballers, totally different from the skinny young boys that seem to have taken over the lower leagues. The athletic looking chaps moved

Big game

freely and pinged the ball about effortlessly. I was still concerned by the amount of high balls, far too many for the top league. As I've mentioned previously, you don't see as many when the teams are playing on artificial surfaces.

The game continued at a higher tempo than before, with Rangers pushing for a winner. It eventually came via an own goal from a Kilmarnock player two minutes from time. The Gers fans set off for home, relieved rather than happy.

I hate trying to get away from Ibrox and the other big stadiums, it's always a nightmare and today was no exception. As I crawled through the traffic and crowd I thought about another stage on this football journey – at the home of one of Scotland's, and indeed Europe's, biggest clubs.

Rangers and Celtic are fish out of water. This is a conclusion that at the outset of this review I probably knew would be confirmed. The sheer scale of the two big boys is incredible compared to the rest. It's only now, after having visited so many of the smaller clubs, that I can start to put it into perspective. Is it time for them to go? Where would they go? Would their departure improve the Scottish leagues?

The sectarian issue is another interesting one. Would it fade if the two clubs had more competition in Scotland? I think it would because currently the Old Firm are blinkered, particularly the supporters. Imagine if there were four or five clubs pushing for the title, do you think all this nonsense about conspiracy theories, bias and hatred would get the same coverage, or would we be talking about Hearts' or Dundee's challenge for the league? If they did go to England or elsewhere, the fans might have more to worry about other than the constant sectarian nonsense that has for so long blighted the game here. More questions than answers. I honestly don't think the profile of Scottish football would be highly regarded if they went completely, there would need to be a compromise such as the Old Firm continuing to play in the Scottish Cup.

I had enjoyed my day at Ibrox but was deeply concerned at the state of affairs at one of the country's biggest clubs. For so long they took the lead in British football but the club has joined the rest in a scrap for survival. Troubled times, and much worse was just around the corner.

Rangers went on to win the league in a nail-biting climax, a new owner and manager bedded themselves in and a number of key players signed extended contracts at the start of season 2011/12. Then the trouble began. The Gers were knocked out of two European competitions at the qualifying stages and lost a League Cup tie to First Division Falkirk. Their league run was papering over the cracks and they were well ahead of stuttering Celtic. Some Rangers players, including Nika Jelavic (who was sold in the January 2012 transfer window), were saying that the title was already in the bag, and it was only October!

Things deteriorated as the festive season approached. Celtic went on an incredible run and were closing in on their great rivals as the Old Firm Ne'er Day derby loomed. The Tic won 1-0 and never looked back while Rangers have been going back the way ever since. Many argue that the origins of the crisis go back much further than this season.

Less than 12 months after my visit to watch Rangers v Kilmarnock, I was back at Ibrox. Kilmarnock were the opposition again, however the situation was completely different. Rangers were in administration and the club was on the brink of extinction – 140 years of history could go down the plug hole. This great institution was on its knees and Scottish football had, arguably, hit its all time low! But as usual, the fans responded and filled the stadium. 'We don't do walking away' was the quote from manager (former player and fan) Ally McCoist. And he's right, the fans never walk away. It's always done by people with no real interest in the clubs beyond self-gain and who are prepared to milk them for every penny. There are also many players who are motivated by money, rather than by love of the game.

The staff and players at Ibrox have displayed commendable loyalty – all have agreed to substantial pay cuts, some as high as 75 per cent, in order to keep the club going. I wonder how many other businesses would experience that level of loyalty.

Numerous Scottish clubs have gone into administration before, so why the furore when it's Rangers? In fact, many long-established businesses have suffered recently due to the global financial meltdown and it is inevitable then that football clubs will suffer as well. The poor financial situation at Rangers has been well documented for years with the banks running the club and the halcyon days of signing players for millions of pounds long gone. Where did it all start to go wrong?

Quote of the day – *Rangers fan, 'The only thing you ever win is best pie competitions.'*

GAME	RANGERS VERSUS KILMARNOCK
DIVISION	SPL
DATE	SUN 13 MAR 2011, KO 3PM
VENUE	IBROX STADIUM, ATTENDANCE 42,417
SCORE	2-1

MATCH STATS:
HTTP://WWW.SCOTPREM.COM/CONTENT/DEFAULT.ASP?PAGE=S13_1_1
&WORKINGDATE=2011-3-13

31

Borderers Overcome the Spiders' Web

WITH PETERHEAD AND BERWICK in my sights, I chose the Borders club and headed north with the wife and pups – making a day of it. Yes, I was heading north, that's the quickest route to the east coast borders from Prestwick. My route took me through Glasgow to Edinburgh and then onto the AI via the city bypass. Two hours and twenty minutes later we were outside the entrance to Shielfield Park. I confirmed arrangements, kissed the better half goodbye and walked towards the stadium for my second instalment between the two teams, the first being at Hampden some six months ago – some contrast.

The sign on the main road indicates both Berwick Rangers and Berwick Speedway and the tight entrance road quickly opened up, with grassland used for parking surrounding the stadium and social club. Multi-purpose stadium are something that I am in favour of but, as with the Blue Brazil's home patch, is motor/bike sport the right option?

The rest of the facilities looked reasonably modern and there was plenty of activity around both the main entrance and the social club. I hovered about, taking some photographs before heading through the only turnstile available and into the second ground in England that I visited during the review, Old Trafford being the other.

On the other side of the turnstile lay the open expanse that is Shielfield Park. Again, memories of Central Park and Hampden (before redevelopment) came flooding back. The place also reminded me of Shawfield; I went there years ago to watch the speedway and also the greyhounds, but never the football. I wondered how good Clyde's pitch was in the 'good old days'. Berwick's looked OK – apart from the most obvious slope seen to date. An artificial pitch would provide a much better playing surface here – no argument whatsoever.

The footprint of the stadium was huge and I was intrigued as to whether this would influence the style of football. The place was busy with supporters congregating for a chat before the game and terraced areas were available. I pondered whether to go outside in the sunshine.

Inquisitive, these Borderers!

Undecided, I went for a look at the menu on the catering van and was pleased to find that Bovril was available (£1.30). The menu, while not brimming with healthy options, offered some welcome alternatives to the usual fare (you can't beat real chips).

I purchased a £2 programme and had a wander through the club shop, placed some bets via the iPhone and then headed up into the stand. I took a seat towards the rear, conscious of the many view-restricting pillars, a common problem with old stadiums. Around me were mostly older folk and some families, all pretty quiet – and this would continue to be the case throughout the game. The smell from the fish and chip van wafted through the air and I could hear east coast mainline trains rumbling by in the distance.

The announcer was giving it big licks, the teams and officials were out – and the referee looked about 14! How would he handle the game, would he get the necessary respect from the players, I wondered. (He did OK, though he was continually harangued from every quarter, 'Back to f**king school, ref' being the phrase of the day. Why are football fans always so critical?)

Sure enough, the openness of the ground did impact on the teams' playing style, with long and high balls the order of the day, which was a shame because the playing surface looked quite good. The game was even for most of the half and the football was nothing much to shout about until a well-taken penalty for the Borderers, and then another on the stroke of half time. Home team 2-0 up at the break. If Queen's got one back early enough, it could make for an entertaining second half.

Half time was spent reading the 'double dunt' programme and chuckling at the announcer, who issued a non-stop stream of instructions to all and sundry. His accent and the crackling tannoy putting me in mind of a ww2 Pathé newsreel voiceover. My thoughts drifted back to the morning, when I had watched fighter jets taking off from Prestwick, for Libya, I assumed. That certainly put things into perspective. Michael Jackson's 'One Day in Your Life' echoed around the stadium.

A few cheers signalled that the teams were out. Queen's Park were definitely playing the better football and got one back 20 minutes into the second half. What a goal – game on! The players were giving their all – while not to the same standard I had witnessed at Ibrox the previous week, their honest endeavour was contributing to a much improved second period. The visiting supporters were increasingly vocal with the young referee the focus for much of their frustrations. The Wee Gers scored again, totally against the run of play, and the game was over as a contest.

As soon as the final whistle sounded, the old tannoy announcer was back, offering congratulations to the team, promoting a '70s disco in the social club and issuing instructions about the forthcoming midweek fixture in Elgin. Elgin! I laughed out loud. Was anybody seriously thinking about this? Why on earth was such a far-flung fixture not scheduled for the weekend and more 'local' ones moved to midweek? The travelling support would be non-existent, some players would probably struggle to get away from work – the whole thing was ludicrous.

On the way home I reflected on Berwick Rangers, an English team playing in the Scottish league. I thought back to the corresponding fixture at Hampden and recalled some racist remarks from the west coast supporters. I'd heard nothing untoward today and had enjoyed my visit. First impressions were favourable, although this is the type of club that I think should have more prominence in the local community and therefore be higher up in the leagues, rather than propping up the Third Division. The club lacked the strong community links evident at places like Forfar and Airdrie, which showed in the pathetic attendance of 398. Where were all the fans? Busy on phone-ins or Facebook, pontificating on the game?

My thoughts turned to the issue of bringing the family along on the football jaunts and how clubs could have 'away match co-ordinators' offering services and information to entice visiting supporters' families to come and spend an afternoon enjoying what the location has to offer, even if not the match itself. Most club websites have details on how to get to the ground but that's about it. What about links to bars and restaurants, town and event guides, what's on, places of interest…

Modern-day supporters expect more.

The drive home seemed to take a long time, probably because the bookie had taken my money again.

Quote of the day – *From all and sundry: 'Back to school, ref!'*

GAME	BERWICK RANGERS VERSUS QUEEN'S PARK
DIVISION	SFL3
DATE	SAT 19 MAR 2011, KO 3PM
VENUE	SHIELFIELD PARK, ATTENDANCE 398
SCORE	3-1

HTTP://WWW.SCOTTISHFOOTBALLLEAGUE.COM/FOOTBALL/THIRD/RESULTS/3284780/

32

THE FIFERS V LIVI LIONS

Livi Roar in Fife

THE DECISION FOR this week's entertainment was a simple one. I had a tutorial in Edinburgh on the Saturday morning so I decided to nip over the Forth Bridge and see the mighty East Fife v Livingston. When I reached Methil I parked in an old industrial estate and sat for a few minutes listening to Radio Scotland. All the talk was of the Brazil friendly the following day at the Emirates. I was annoyed that I hadn't managed to get down there. I did mention the possibility to the better half, my tack being that it would be good to go to Arsenal's new stadium; she quickly replied that I had already been there to see Rangers a few seasons ago, and that's as far as I got. Like most Scotland supporters, my last memory of Brazil was in Paris in 1998. Myself and some friends thought that we had secured tickets for the opening day encounter with the then reigning world champions, only to be let down at the last minute. But the travel agency was absolutely fantastic: as they had already chartered the plane, they flew us to Paris and back, and gave us a full refund – does that kind of thing happen anymore?

Arguably, that was the best flight I've ever been on (the competition being one from the former Yugoslavia in 1991 just before all hell broke loose after Scotland played in San Marino). The British Caledonian (remember them?) DC10 was bouncing all the way to Paris even though the SFA had allegedly imposed a booze ban. Champagne, whisky and just about everything else was being passed around as soon as the seat belt signs went off and the atmosphere was fantastic. And who could forget the few minutes during that brilliant game when we equalised. I had a feeling that we were going to beat Brazil – now that's what football's all about, living the dream!

On the radio, Joe Jordan was reminiscing about world cups, tales of the great players and teams rolling off his tongue. The presenters were also thinking back to the top TV moments from the '70s, '80s and '90s. Just being part of the greatest show on earth is fantastic. And then suddenly everything came crashing down to earth when Billy Dodds commented that he had nothing to talk about regarding major tournaments! This dynamic centre forward gave his heart and soul for the country but unfortunately like so many of his generation never made it to a major championship. That's the reality of Scottish football at the moment, we are merely making up the numbers in a truly global phenomenon and we need to get back to the top table – this must be the aim for everyone involved in our national sport.

Among fans from both teams I made my way towards the stadium, looking for the main entrance and a photo opportunity. With no main sign to be found, I went into the club shop and purchased a programme before deciding to join the visitors' end for the day, primarily because it was nearer to the car and I would get a flier. The usual turnstile manoeuvre was undertaken, £13 was handed over and I entered Bayview for the first time.

First act was toilets and then I joined the queue for some food. Service was swift and friendly and I was soon munching on an excellent steak pie (got my appetite back for them), washed down with a delicious Bovril. Possibly the best food yet. The standard menu was augmented with an abundance of chocolate bars. I carried on through the tunnel (I like grounds with tunnels leading out into the main arena, it feels like you're running out onto the pitch) and up into the stand, again choosing an end-of-row seat. The solitary stand looked directly onto a big chimney, part of an old industrial complex. The place reminded me of Cappielow with its relics of yesteryear, except that the Fifers seemed to be part of a general regeneration, unlike the Greenock Morton. Four big floodlight poles towered over a reasonable looking pitch. All in all, the set-up looked pretty good.

Teams out, iPhone logged onto BBC football.

The early period of the game was disappointing, lots of high balls and generally pretty scrappy. The Fife began to get a grip on the game (much to the annoyance of the healthy Livi support, except for one gent behind me who clapped and cheered every good move, no matter which team produced it). They were unlucky to go behind against the run of play. Livingston are a good side and know how to win football matches, but the home side kept at it. Their joint endeavours were producing a right good game, particularly when the ball was played on the deck. Incidentally, this strategy should also save the club some money on lost footballs as three disappeared in the first half alone.

The first half concluded with the visitors one up and the fans getting colder. I wondered why the stand hadn't been built facing away from the sea to give some shelter from the breeze. The match programme provided some interesting reading during the break, a certain Mr Durie (former East Fife, Hibs, Spurs, Rangers...) mentioned first as coach and then as a young player on the East Fife subs bench in a 1982 encounter against Meadowbank Thistle, the Livingston of old. Another feature discussed the average attendance figures for the clubs in the division. Only Ayr and Livi were showing more than 1,000 with the rest on or around the 500 mark. That worried me. Surely we can encourage more people to these games, something is not right.

The teams re-entered the stadium and I again focused my attention on the playing arena, which was surrounded by advertising signs; as in Forfar, it was evident that someone in marketing was doing a right good job.

Livingston upped the ante but the Fifers weren't beat yet and scored against the run of play. From a neutral's point of view it was all good entertainment and kept one's mind off the chilly breeze. Livi's quest to overcome the stubborn Fifers continued and they went on to score another two very good goals, emphasising their class, and closed the game out methodically with another three points in the bag (they were promoted as champions a couple of weeks later).

Bayview Stadium is modern and in an area that is developing. The club are considering artificial turf for both the main and training pitches. The youth set-up looks very interesting, with the award winning East Fife juniors and the recently announced modern apprenticeship schemes for 12 promising young players. This really emphasises how strong links with the community can bring dividends as many local people and businesses are investing in and supporting the club. The stadium is a bit of a walk from the town (in my perfect world it would be closer) and therefore much work needs to be done to attract the locals to spend

Must be for the five-a-sides!

an afternoon or evening there. However, this club has a bit of life about it and has a good infrastructure, two key ingredients for survival.

Quote of the day – *Elderly chap behind me: 'Bloody good show!' Everything he said was positive, encouraging and impartial – a real breath of fresh air, so much better than the usual drivel.*

GAME	EAST FIFE VERSUS LIVINGSTON
DIVISION	SFL2
DATE	SAT 26 MAR 2011, KO 3PM
VENUE	BAYVIEW STADIUM, ATTENDANCE 707
SCORE	1-3

MATCH STATS:
HTTP://WWW.SCOTTISHFOOTBALLLEAGUE.COM/FOOTBALL/SECOND/
RESULTS/3284820/

33

THE STAGGIES V THE PARS

Parry Parry Night

NON-STOP NOW TILL the end of the season – two games a week – and Dingwall the destination for game 33. I had managed to organise some work in the area to coincide with the fixture and was staying overnight at the National Hotel near Victoria Park. After dumping my gear in my room I went downstairs to stoke up. Curry demolished (it reminded me of the meals at the shipyard canteen – great expectations, then disappointment) and a few beers downed, it was time to experience my first game in the Highlands.

After a five-minute stroll I was in amongst the faithful outside the Main Stand – gaun the Staggies! After purchasing a £16 ticket at a portacabin, I wandered around outside for a wee while, taking photographs and generally getting a feel for the place. One thing I'd noticed over the season was the amount of 'Save Our Club' campaigns and this one was 'Save Our Staggies'. Another sign announced Ross County as 'More Than Just a Football Club' – and so they should be, a club like the Staggies should take centre stage in the local community and I wondered just how prominent they were. To date, my analysis would place clubs like RC in a favourable position, limited local competition, good stadium and other facilities close by and recent history suggested a club on the rise, all the makings of an excellent community organisation.

Among the usual merchandise at the club shop, one item caught my eye: Frank Gilfeather's *Ross County: From Highland League to Hampden*, a book that sits proudly on many shelves and is testament to a magnificent achievement in season 2009/10.

After handing over my ticket to the turnstile attendant (why the unnecessary trip to the ticket office?), I entered the foyer where there is an interesting array of pictures of teams, past and present. The

Save them?

snack bars were doing a roaring trade (a Snickers and a Bovril for me tonight) and the people milling around were talking all things football. In the stand I had some difficulty finding my very cramped back row seat but after some confusion I squeezed myself into the evening's pew and settled down.

The place was filling up nicely but there wasn't much in terms of atmosphere. Adjacent to the stadium, again under floodlights, were some artificial pitches and I couldn't help but think that the game would be much better if played over there rather on the rough looking surface that was in front of me. Anyway, not to worry, it promised to be a good game what with Dunfermline chasing promotion and Ross County, now under the guidance of the excitable Jimmy Calderwood, trying desperately for points so as to avoid the drop. The PA fell silent.

Unfortunately, there was no roar to signal the start of the game, just a few cheers and words of encouragement for the players. (Later there was a roar in the distance, the sound of fighter jets in the sky and as usual football was firmly put into perspective for me with the thought of events in the Middle East.)

Both teams tried to get a grip on things early on with Dunfermline edging the opening proceedings. Not a lot of quality on show, lots of high balls and commitment but few chances at either end. The status quo was sustained until half time. The main event in the first half had been Calderwood's crazy rant at the linesman – just as well the cameras weren't there!

The programme yielded nothing of major interest and my thoughts moved elsewhere. I noticed the Highland Football Academy adjacent

A dusky Victoria Park

to the stadium and that the ground was packed with advertising, including encouragement to get involved online – all great stuff.

The mediocre football continued until midway through the second half when the Staggies started playing a bit better. Their improved performance levels weren't matched by enthusiasm on the terraces and the place remained quiet. With both rain and the temperature falling, I had started looking forward to a few beers back in the warm hotel when all of a sudden the game came to life. The visitors seriously upped the ante, chances were created and incredibly missed, the game ebbed and flowed and then there was a killer blow for the home side. Dunfermline (a team that I have never been impressed with) scored in injury time. The Dingwallians were as gutted as the Pars' tiny travelling support were delighted.

Back in the hotel bar, I mulled over the night's proceedings over a few beers. My thoughts were that Ross County should be OK for the future; good set-up and great potential.

Fast forward 12 months and the club are entering the Premier League – which brings other challenges, most notably the fact that Victoria Park doesn't meet SPL standards and the standing areas will need to be converted to all-seated arrangements, which will be costly. In the meantime, a ground-sharing arrangement with Inverness may need to be implemented, which seems ridiculous to me – safe standing areas should be perfectly acceptable in the top league. That aside, chairman Roy McGregor's vision, following the model developed by Ipswich Town, is coming to fruition. Ipswich Town's community-focused approach increased attendances and now a tenth of the local community regularly watch the Tractor Boys. McGregor told the BBC: 'If more clubs looked towards their relationship with their community, it would be better for their football. That's where football came from, and if football is to survive in today's market, it's going to have to work closer with its community.'

Interesting and exciting times lie ahead for the Staggies.

Quote of the day – *Wee Staggies fan. 'Dad, why's it always freezing when we come here?'*

GAME	ROSS COUNTY VERSUS DUNFERMLINE
DIVISION	SFL1
DATE	TUES 29 MAR 2011, KO 7.45PM
VENUE	VICTORIA PARK, ATTENDANCE 2,059
SCORE	0-1

MATCH STATS:
HTTP://WWW.SCOTTISHFOOTBALLLEAGUE.COM/FOOTBALL/FIRST/
RESULTS/3370336/

34

THE GABLE ENDIES V THE BLACK & WHITES

Missing Links for Elgin

I REJECTED POTENTIAL venues McDiarmid and Starks Park in favour of Montrose, the furthest away one for the weekend sortie. Three hours (I'm mad) after leaving Prestwick I was parked on Union Place on an absolutely glorious afternoon. My impression of the town remembered from years gone by was of a dreary place with not much going on – but this time around it was busy and generally had a good feel to it.

I arrived pretty jaded after the long drive and the absolute nonsense I'd listened to on the radio. *Off* and *On the Ball* infuriated me with a nonsensical debate between two of the commentators on the 'Did he? Didn't he?' interview with Rangers chairman Alastair Johnston. Please note, absolutely no talk about football.

The journey was uneventful, apart from all the Celtic supporters' buses and coaches stopping on the opposite carriageway for toilet breaks! Their early kick-off game at Inverness had been called off at short notice due to a waterlogged pitch and they were now heading home. On the radio Peter Lawell, Celtic's chief executive, was complaining about the scheduling, but the clubs agree to this regime when they accept the TV money. And what about the fans? When are they ever consulted?

Time for the football. Links Park lies at the end of a short cul-de-sac. Halfway down there is a social club and a few lads were departing with rosy glows on their cheeks! There was plenty of parking available all the way round to the Main Stand which, side on, reminded me of Pac Man (an early '80s video game). A small but no doubt very useful walled artificial pitch lay towards the end of stand, next to derelict looking away supporters' turnstiles. I chuckled at the dedicated 'Manager's Parking' spot.

At the turnstile, £10 (great value) gets you into a covered section

Training pitch – no escape!

with the club shop and other facilities. Programme purchased, I walked round to the snack bar (typical menu) and purchased my 'usual' steak pie (£1.60) and Bovril (70p, and climbed high up into the steep stand, which reminded me of Tynecastle. I took in the great view, watched the distant wind turbines for a while, and primed the iPhone for the day's football scores. The PA was barely audible, presumably due to the close proximity of the houses that surround the park. There was a real family atmosphere and everyone was eagerly anticipating the teams coming out to start the game. However, in typical Third Division fashion, the teams were a few minutes late in coming out – real fitba'!

The ball was soon whizzing about, mostly on the deck, and both teams were trying to play football. It struck me that there was no chance the ICT v Celtic game would have been called off if the stadium had had an artificial pitch like the one here.

The game was pretty even until the home side took the lead with a good header. The temptation to launch the ball forward still afflicts many players and there was a spell when a few big kicks up the park took precedence when other options may have been more fruitful. However, the game was generally played on the carpet with lots of good

PacMan

skill, particularly from the Elgin No. 9, and the odd miss-kick, one of which was easily 'Miss of the Season'. There was a minor incident as half time approached but the linesman was quick to intervene and the handbags were put back in the cupboard. Home side one up, much to the delight of the 'blue rinsed' Montrose young supporters.

I settled down with the highly entertaining 'Gable Ender' programme during the break – lots of reading about the club and football in general, great value at £1.50. There was also mention of how the club was struggling.

Elgin came racing out of the blocks and started having a real go early doors. Eventually the Gable Endies got back into it but couldn't increase their lead due to some woeful finishing. A couple of Montrose fans were singing away happily (they'd probably had one too many), but in terms of atmosphere that was the highlight. The game itself was petering out, the quality dropped and more chances were missed. Elgin's female physio bounced onto the park near the end to treat a player and that was almost the last piece of action – time for home.

I had enjoyed my first visit to Links Park. There is definitely a trend developing in terms of the type of football club that I prefer and

Montrose fits the bill. Again though, I was concerned by the lack of numbers at the game – under 300. I had expected more fans at the game in this reasonably busy port town.

Is a radical overhaul of Scottish football required if crowds are ever to increase again – I think so.

Further research revealed very little in the way of the community links that have been so successful for clubs of a similar ilk. There is a recognised youth set-up which is always encouraging. However, I feel more could be done with the local community. The artificial pitches are a definite plus point and should be marketed accordingly, along with the modern facilities within the stadium. Dedicated fans were staffing the club shops and stalls – maybe it's time for a community interest club arrangement for the Gable Endies!

Quote of the day – *Drunk Montrose fan: We're gonnae win the league!'*

GAME	MONTROSE VERSUS ELGIN CITY
DIVISION	SFL3
DATE	SAT 2 APRIL 2011, KO 3PM
VENUE	LINKS PARK STADIUM, ATTENDANCE 256
SCORE	I-0

MATCH STATS:
HTTP://WWW.SCOTTISHFOOTBALLLEAGUE.COM/FOOTBALL/THIRD/
RESULTS/3284892/

35

THE SAINTS V THE GERS

Early KOS not OK

I WAS IN EDINBURGH on business and as the day wore on, the 6 o'clock kick off at Perth edged St Johnstone for today's match – the unusually early kick off meant that I would get home at a reasonable hour after a long day. I checked ticketing arrangements and was assured there would be a public sale up until the match got under way and that the car park was open as usual. I had been to McDiarmid Park before, but only for business meetings, and I was looking forward to seeing a game in a stadium that reminded me of Ibrox, from the inside anyway. The parking attendant had to be paid first though, and £3 was handed over for the pleasure. In terms of value, this would be decided on exit – I don't mind paying if the arrangements to get back on the road are swift and hassle free.

The place was much busier than the lower league games I'd been attending recently. Spotting a few familiar faces, I felt at 'home' in Perth and was enjoying the atmosphere already. I left the ticket office £20 lighter and joined the Gers faithful at the Ormond Stand turnstiles (once more, why not just have a pay turnstile?). Never mind, the metal cage clicked, I was inside the stand and immediately facing me was the programme seller. Another £2.50 was handed over, running total £25.50, not including fuel. It was time for the snack bar and this evening's dinner. There was a reasonable choice, including chicken fajitas and meal deals, but I plumped for the usual steak pie (good) Bovril and crisps, and a KitKat as well – greedy boy!

I had no idea of team line-ups, in fact I didn't even know that the Partick Thistle game had been called off due to a waterlogged pitch. Just as well I'd headed north. Programme, pie and Bovril in hand, crisps and chocolate bar in the pocket, I headed out into the stand and located my seat.

The modern McDiarmid Park

McDiarmid Park, in my opinion, is almost perfect in terms of set-up. The only downside is that it's a fair walk from the city centre. The facilities for the football side of things looked good with adjacent artificial pitches and excellent business facilities within the stadium. Pity the main playing surface was such a mess – again, an artificial pitch would be the answer. The stadium could have done with a roof as the wind was howling through the gaps between the four stands.

The game was pretty even in the early stages with both teams seemingly unwilling to keep the ball on the deck. The visitors got the breakthrough after a mistake by a Saints defender and the Ormond Stand erupted as the ball hit the back of the net just in front of me. The goal was all about speed, which is the key difference between the leagues. The players in the top division look much healthier and fitter than their counterparts in the lower divisions. Unfortunately, the same can't be said for the quality of the football. This game wasn't good on the eye, particularly with Rangers now clearly dominating. The first half ended without further excitement – time for a read of the programme.

I started with the column by manager Derek McInnes and was immediately confused: 'I am writing these notes before we travel to Celtic Park on Boxing Day,' I read. Incredibly, the programme was nearly four months out of date and was actually printed for the visit of Rangers and Inverness CT on 29/12/10 and 02/01/11 respectively. Now I know things are tight but this was totally out of order and I felt cheated. When I look back in years to come this programme will not properly reflect the time when I visited Perth. The 'History Book' section was interesting, but all this season's stats were out of date – poor show.

The large fir trees behind the opposite stand were swaying vigorously, a sign that the wind was picking up. During the second half the ball seemed to be in the air a lot, which doesn't make for a good game. The electronic scoreboard continued to display 1-0 to the visitors until deep into the half when Rangers doubled their lead and the game as a contest was over.

On the road home, the night's Champions League action on the radio, I thought back over the day's experience. The stadium was modern and inviting, everything was in place for a successful club, yet there were less than 6,000 fans at the match. OK, the kick-off time might have been a factor, but that would have had more of a bearing on the travelling support. St Johnstone's nearest rivals are about 20 miles away and you would imagine that this fixture would attract more local people. If the Saints can't get more fans through the gates with the infrastructure they have in place, what chance have the rest of the clubs got? On the other hand, if the non Old Firm clubs had a realistic chance of winning the league or the Scottish Cup, it seems likely more fans would turn up.

I agree with BBC pundit Jim Spence who I have heard arguing the relationship between competition and attendance figures. He referred back to the halcyon post-war days of season 1948/49 when Dundee, Aberdeen and Hibs were pulling in over 20,000 spectators every week and Rangers pipped Dundee (yes Dundee) for the title by one point. In 1950 Rangers again nabbed the top spot, one point ahead of Hibs, who were followed by Hearts, East Fife, then Celtic – fascinating stuff.

Yes, I know it was just after the war and there was a feel-good factor and less to do leisure-wise, but times were much tougher. Celtic and Rangers were still a good bit ahead but nothing like the way it is today. They've become far too powerful and this has been to the detriment of the Scottish game ever since they

Lights, camera action

started dominating in the mid-'80s.

The other ten clubs in the SPL recognise this and at time of writing moves are afoot to address the imbalance. However, immediately the SFA's proposal to create a new national league was made public, the Old Firm let it be known that they would oppose this; on top of which, Duff and Phelps, the administrators at Rangers, must be acutely aware that any such move might dissuade prospective buyers. It really is a difficult situation. The Old Firm are unlikely to agree to anything that could weaken their businesses, that's understandable, but the game is crying out for more competition. Unless the big two move on or relinquish some of their power, a renaissance looks extremely unlikely.

Quote of the day – *Rangers fan: 'I gave up time and half to watch this pish!'*

GAME	ST JOHNSTONE VERSUS RANGERS
DIVISION	SPL
DATE	TUES 5 APR 2011, KO 6PM
VENUE	MCDIARMID PARK, ATTENDANCE 5,820
SCORE	0-2

MATCH STATS:
HTTP://WWW.SCOTPREM.COM/CONTENT/DEFAULT.ASP?PAGE=S97_1_1 &WORKINGDATE=2011-4-5

36

THE CITY V THE FIFERS

Hot in the City for Brechin

FOR TODAY'S FIXTURES I consulted the *Daily Record* and basically I had two choices, Brechin or Raith. My concentration on deciding on the day's football was lost for a while when I started reading the preview for Hamilton v Rangers, – it was totally focused on sectarianism. What's it all about! Anyway, I chose Brechin because it was furthest away and started planning for my day out in Angus after looking at my favourite 'Punter' section.

Having had a few beers the previous evening, I was feeling a bit rough. Throw into the mix a wife who was getting a wee bit fed up about being left alone Saturday after Saturday and an ever-sprouting garden that desperately needed my attention, and it's understandable that the motivation was a bit low at the outset. However, two and a half hours later, I was parked on the main road outside Glebe Park and I was keenly anticipating my day at the fitba', possibly because I'd been listening to *Off the Ball* on the journey and the show had fielded a selection of guests that really appealed to me.

A representative of Albion Rovers spoke passionately about involving clubs in the local community – and of course I totally agreed with him. Growing organically is the way forward, good luck to the Albion.

Another guest was trying to revive Third Lanark, which amazed me. He and his mate worked at night and at weekends restoring Cathkin Park the home of the now defunct Third Lanark (the name has been adopted by a local team). The long-term aim was to re-establish the club as a force in Scottish football – how good is that? This country is mad about the game for all the right reasons, pity we can't rid ourselves of the sectarian nonsense. The show's third guest was a female professional footballer, plying her trade in Germany and

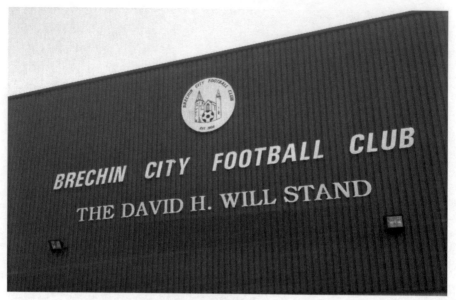

FIFA's Mr Will

thoroughly enjoying the experience. She mentioned the high quality facilities available over there.

What would Brechin have to offer? Anyway, more important stuff to worry about. The afternoon's investments had to be made so the iPhone was brought into action and the bets placed.

A track with residential dwellings on either side led down to the stadium; all very pleasant. I had the iPhone out again to take some pictures and one of the female hi-viz brigade looked most taken aback, obviously thinking I was taking a photograph of her. I handed over £12 to the friendly turnstile woman and entered Glebe Park for the first time. The imposing David Will Stand immediately confronts all supporters, a timely reminder of Scottish football's place at the heart of world football. I remember Mr Will being second in command at FIFA for a while. It's just a pity Scotland is not second in the international standings – dream on!

Once I was inside I explored for a while, then headed for the programme vendor and on to the snack bar located at the corner of the stand, where you get a good view of the pitch. The set-up put me in mind of a bowling club – there was a high hedge on one side and opposite, the very traditional stand-cum-clubhouse – all very quaint. Shock horror, no steak pies, only Scotch pies on sale. No way was I risking another Fir Park incident, so I plumped for a sausage roll and Bovril (both very good) and decided to sit high up in the David Will Stand for the views across the countryside, but my seat was in the shade and a chilly breeze made it less of a pleasure.

The teams appeared at about three minutes past three and duly changed ends. This action confirmed that I was sitting in the away end as the Brechin fans in the terrace opposite started streaming towards me, presumably expecting a goal fest for the home side. Last time I'd seen Brechin was on the first day of the season at Somerset Park and I'd been reasonably impressed by them. They'd started the season well and were in a good position in the league for the early part but had slipped somewhat in recent months. Today's visitors were on a bit of a roll and it had all the makings of a good game; pity that the pitch looked so rough.

The ref blew his whistle and the usual hurlyburly ensued before the teams settled and started playing football. Chances were missed at both ends. It was pleasing to see the ball on the deck – most of the time. As the game ebbed and flowed, I noticed that the officious stewards kept pestering youngsters. The healthy travelling support were getting behind their team, definitely a lot more vocal than the home lot. With honours even at half time I decided to relocate, via the toilet (no hot water or soap), to the sunshine and took up a position close to the away dugout. I leant against the barrier reading the interesting programme with the sun on my back for the rest of the break period – great to get a heat.

Teams out for the second half and the supporters had shifted positions once again. The visitors took the lead, much to the disappointment of the home fans and myself. My bookie will be happy! East Fife scored again (actually a Brechin OG), but Brechin got one back. You would be forgiven for thinking that there was hope, but deep down I wasn't convinced, and rightly so, as East Fife added to their tally with a deserved third.

Great entertainment, two teams committed to winning the game and a couple of really good goals as well. All in all an enjoyable afternoon, particularly the second half, spent in the sunshine with the occasional waft of cigar smoke.

I had enjoyed my day, except for some of the results. In the car my attention turned to Brechin and their place in the overall scheme of Scottish football. They are a club that have spent the majority of their history in the lower leagues and this is disappointing. Even with the inspirational leadership of David Will, they failed to maintain

First Division status for long and returned almost immediately to their Second Division comfort zone.

I can't resist making the comparison with Ross County. There's no reason why Brechin couldn't do something similar with a bit of fire in their bellies! Yes, there are differences in their circumstances. Angus has many clubs in a small area and therefore more competition exists, not only for supporters, but for investment and sponsorship etc. But every cloud has a silver lining. Brechin could get together with Montrose, Forfar and Arbroath, share administration and other business functions, look at community issues and work together for the good of football in Angus as a whole, to the benefit of all concerned. And I noticed that Angus Council recently became involved in a partnership with the SFA and has appointed its own officer to develop football in the community – good stuff.

Brechin should use Ross County as the benchmark and believe that it can be done. There's no point in moaning about having no money, everyone is struggling. They could also turn for inspiration to Youth Football Scotland, a shining example of how to organise regionally, manage and play the game in a professional manner. They offer a pool of resources from advice on healthy eating, to sports science, to finding a pitch – I'm certain that the senior clubs, not only those in Angus, could learn from this co-ordinated approach.

Quote of the day – *Third Lanark fan on the radio: 'We are trying to establish the club as a force in Scottish football again.' Amazing!*

GAME	BRECHIN CITY VERSUS EAST FIFE
DIVISION	SFL2
DATE	SAT 9 APRIL 2011, KO 3PM
VENUE	GLEBE PARK, ATTENDANCE 504
SCORE	1-3

MATCH STATS:
HTTP://WWW.SCOTTISHFOOTBALLLEAGUE.COM/FOOTBALL/SECOND/
RESULTS/3284952/

37

THE JAGS V THE BAIRNS

A Jag Fae the Bairns

GAME 37, DESTINATION Firhill, my first visit here for many a year. I was looking forward to it. There's something very 'olde worlde' about the Main Stand that I like. The place already had a football feel to it when I arrived, way too early, at 6.15 (KO 7.45), and parked on Northpark Street. There were plenty of police and stewards directing traffic and enforcing the no-parking zones, unlike many of the other smaller grounds I had visited recently where you hardly see a policeman and traffic cones are few and far between – this is real football – west coast style.

I passed some time flicking between the various local and national radio stations, all broadcasting the same topic – football. The coverage is incessant, particularly when the Old Firm are involved and the 'shame game' was still high on everyone's agenda – give it a rest! The other main talking point was Celtic's early kick off in Perth and the fans protesting by kicking balls over the stands and onto the pitch during the game.

My view is that visiting fans are essential to the atmosphere and every effort should be made to suit the convenience of the majority. I'm sure that would be reflected in the attendance.

Car locked and double-checked (Maryhill isn't the most salubrious of Glasgow's suburbs), and within a few hundred yards the floodlights and the old Main Stand were in full view. There was plenty of activity, the club shop was busy, as were the lounges overlooking the street. Much too my disappointment, none of the Main Stand turnstiles were open and further enquiries revealed that I would be sitting in the Jackie Husband Stand, opposite my favourite Maryhill perch.

I headed round the corner and up the hill, purchasing a programme

The way it used to be

(only £1 but out of date) and passing some remnants of a bygone age. The barriers for the old (south) terrace were still visible, a stark reminder of how football stadiums used to be – up and over – stairs up and then down again towards the pitch. It brought back memories of going to the football as a youngster in an era when it seemed busier and noisier. Tonight it was calm, quiet and relaxed – expectations were probably not what they used to be. My stop at the ticket portacabin left me £17 lighter (I noticed that entry for kids was free), I went through the turnstile, handed over my ticket (now what was the point of that), and found myself in the spacious foyer. At the snack bar I bought a steak pie (£2) and Bovril (£1.60), both good, and a sneaky packet of crisps and a Twix.

I chose a seat high up and proceeded to devour my evening meal, savouring the views across Glasgow and looking towards where I really wanted to be – the old Main Stand. The pitch was in a horrendous state, loads of brown and bare patches – the worst yet. The pitches at Berwick and St Johnstone were bad but this was on another level, or bump, to be more precise. I'm led to believe that the damage is caused by ground sharing with Glasgow Warriors Rugby Club. While I'm a staunch advocate of multi-use facilities, that's not the case when it's to the detriment of the games involved. Artificial turf could have coped with the rigours of lots of matches, but this old patch just wasn't up to it.

Fortunately, there was better viewing available inside the stadium. The good weather had brought out the lassies, some crackers as well

– what a welcome change! There were lots of families present, which was good to see, and the usual old-timers who had probably seen it all umpteen times before – what keeps them coming back, week in, week out, season after season? As kick off approached, stewards buzzed around stewarding, the cheers and shouts were getting louder and the atmosphere was building – game on in Maryhill!

'Slow' is the best way to describe the majority of the first half but at least the ball was being played on the deck. The home crowd, the noisiest in recent weeks, were giving vent to loads of negative drivel with Falkirk manager Stephen Pressley on the receiving end of much of the abuse. There wasn't much in terms of a response from the away support (numbering only about a hundred and that's being generous), which was disappointing because the Bairns still had a lot to play for. The first half was pretty even but low on quality, and I was glad when it petered out and I got the chance to stand up for a while. It had grown chillier. The sun sank and the floodlights took over lighting duties.

This was another occasion that the programme was out of date, by nearly two months (at least they only charged £1) and it was pretty pointless spending time reading it. A match programme really captures a moment in time and when they are out of date they lose so much of their value. Anyway, there were far more interesting things to look at. The Firhill 'doocot' situated on the unused south terrace is the most bizarre feature in any of the Scottish senior grounds, the Main Stand is a classic and the clock that stops after 40 minutes on the North Stand is another,. And, as I mentioned earlier, the views over Glasgow from where I was sitting were excellent, something you don't get in the old Main.

Teams out for the second half, both going for it from the whistle. The Jags edged the opening stages and the lively start got the fans going. After a few missed chances for the home side, the Bairns opened the scoring and took the wind from the Jags' sails. Insults started flying towards Thistle manager Ian McCall and increased exponentially when Falkirk doubled their lead. The writing was on the wall for the home side and the full-time whistle couldn't come soon enough, even a late goal couldn't efface the disappointment of the fans, including myself. Another First Division game low on quality. What is it about the second tier of Scottish football?

On the road home I reflected that this was the second time I'd seen Thistle this season and the second time I'd been disappointed with them. Last time they were well beaten by Stirling Albion in a much

Why is my favourite Maryhill perch closed?

better game than tonight's. Although relegation wasn't a threat, the 'safe' mid-table position does nothing to ignite passion among the fans or players. And the out-of-date programme indicated that, like many others, Partick Thistle are struggling.

So many senior clubs are teetering on the brink of financial collapse. If they are being artificially kept afloat, I don't think that is doing the game any good. A recent survey of Championship Leagues 1 and 2, carried out by a leading firm of administrators, highlights the fact that nearly one in five clubs south of the border are financially distressed, principally due to expenditure on players' wages. That 19 per cent compares to just one per cent in the wider economy. Living beyond your means will eventually come back and haunt you – a quick glance at the austerity measures being enforced throughout Europe confirms this.

However, there is hope, and as usual, the fans are trying their utmost to get things going again. The Jagettes, a group of female Thistle fans, are conducting a 'social experiment' to boost football attendances by fitting the game around what they describe as a 'girly day out'. As their leader, Marie-Claire Palmer, explains: 'Partick do a great job in letting children under-16 in for free for League games and they have a support of about 2,000 that is mostly blokes. It dawned on me that they had never specifically targeted the female market.'

How right she is. On my tour round Scottish grounds I can only remember one other specific advertisement for females and that was a Ladies Night at Stenhousemuir. All moves to draw in women are particularly timely now that the women's game is going from strength to strength.

I always like what fresh eyes can bring to a situation and the Jagettes could potentially be the freshest yet. The sport is male-dominated throughout. I personally never thought about the influence women could have – very interesting.

Quote of the day – *Thistle fan: 'Come away the Partick Thistle!' (Took me back – my granny's budgie used to say this.)*

GAME	PARTICK THISTLE VERSUS FALKIRK
DIVISION	SFL1
DATE	TUES 12 APRIL 2011, KO 7.45PM
VENUE	FIRHILL, ATTENDANCE 1,142
SCORE	1-2

MATCH STATS:
HTTP://WWW.SCOTTISHFOOTBALLLEAGUE.COM/FOOTBALL/FIRST/RESULTS/3384842/

38

THE RED LICHTIES V THE SPIDERS

Smokin' in Arbroath

THREE EXTRA PASSENGERS – wife and pups in the vehicle for the trip to Angus. No *Off the Ball* on the radio as Stuart and Tam's teams were playing in the semi-final of the Scottish Cup in the early kick off at Hampden where Motherwell were reported to be in total control. My 'investments' for the day were looking good. When we reached Arbroath my passengers set off for a walk along the coast and I made my way to the ground. The Tutties Neuk was doing a roaring trade and it was good to see plenty of Spiders fans enjoying the hospitality. There really was a good atmosphere around the place, very easygoing, I felt like I was on holiday.

It was a pleasure handing the friendly turnstile attendant a modest £12 to get into the game. The ground reminded me of a farm courtyard – the turnstiles looked like stables with the Main Stand a big farmhouse, but I liked it, there was something quaint about the whole place. However, in terms of business efficiency, I wondered how the old stadium performed.

First stop was the snack bar and for £3.20 I managed to get a steak pie and a Bovril – both OK. Next purchase was the match programme and then I wandered around the terraces for a while before settling on a position in the southeast corner. Just over the wall was the sea. It doesn't get much better than that – glorious.

There was a good turnout of visiting fans, some in Hawaiian shirts (I'm sure I clocked the guy who runs the club shop for the Spiders at Hampden). I overheard a couple of guys talking about the round of golf they'd had at Carnoustie before the game. Now that's what I call a real day out – participating in sport, watching football and then downing a few in the evening. Plenty of singing was to be heard from

Gayfield in the sun

both sets of fans and things were developing nicely for what looked like being an interesting game – Arbroath could win the league if results went their way.

The teams ran out onto a great looking pitch, to the *Match of the Day* theme tune – brilliant – then 'Yellow Submarine' was blasted out – game on at Gayfield! Both teams came flying out the traps, probably at too high a tempo. At first this affected the quality of the game – the ball was in the air quite a lot, surprising, because it was quite breezy. Things eventually settled down and the quality of football improved with the Red Lichties taking control. But as so often happens, the goal came against the run of play, much to the delight of the vociferous Glaswegian supporters. Their lead didn't last long as the home side equalised from an excellent free kick and the half finished all square. Good game so far and much to look forward to in the second half.

Half time was spent admiring the views, browsing the programme and checking the scores on the iPhone – the coupon was looking good, I needed Arbroath to make it a great afternoon though. The programme was sparse but at only £1.50 that was to be expected. A few articles caught my eye with the one claiming that Scotsmen were instrumental in introducing football to Brazil the most intriguing.

Reading the programme had taken my mind off the weather and when I finished I was glad I could move around to warm up. I imagined that winter games at Gayfield Park would be quite a challenge, a surmise that I later confirmed via an online search: 'On stormy winter days, waves beat on the walls surrounding the ground. Clearances in the teeth of the gale, let alone polished football, become impossible. Goalkeepers can find it hard to spot the ball to kick out and even then goalkicks occasionally fly out for corners. Throw in the ubiquitous seagulls and, inclement weather, the rides on Pleasureland next door, and Gayfield offers a unique, bracing and surreal spectacle with wonderful views when the game pales.' In summary, don't expect to see the beautiful game here in winter. We need people to be brave and make a stand for March to November (Marvember) football – I'm dreaming again, it will never happen!

The Carpenters 'Top of the World' was playing over the PA and I was singing along when the teams came back out. The home fans had moved en masse and had joined me at the south side of the ground. Meanwhile, my fellow Glaswegians had taken the opposite route and had decamped to the north. Everything was in place for a good half and what a half it turned out to be.

Arbroath scored right after the restart and continued to play excellent football throughout. Chances aplenty were created, and spurned, by the league leaders with their No. 10, Swankie, orchestrating most of the good play. The Lichties were on top and my other results were looking good as well, it could be a rewarding day. And then, again, Queen's scored against the run of play, unbelievable, but great entertainment, although the home support must have been at their wits end. After a superb second half performance from the Maroons, the great game finished a 2-2 draw.

Arbroath had drawn but my other results had come in, so not bad re the investments. I set off down to the harbour to meet up with the wife and enjoy the best fish supper we'd tasted for a while.

When driving past Gayfield Park, I'd thought it was a real dump. How wrong I was. Now it was definitely on my list of favourite stadiums. The drive south gave me plenty of time to reflect on what had been a very enjoyable day.

As is often the case, I would have expected more of the locals to turn out to support their team, especially when they could have won the league. The stadium itself is dated but well maintained and in good order. It seemed right for the fans – an all-seated version wouldn't suit them (other clubs and organisations should take note of the fact that they're not for everyone). However, the stadium could be used for little else, that's one of the downsides of these older buildings. There didn't seem to be any other facilities for the players close by but the playing surface looked too good to be used for training as well, so I assumed the club had other arrangements.

The future looks OK for this friendly seaside club. Promotion was achieved the week after my visit and the fans could look forward to seeing different teams for at least a season. Promotion and relegation are essential ingredients in the football mix, it's healthy; we should have more teams going up and down through the leagues. My main worry for the Lichties is the concentration of clubs in the area – Forfar, Brechin, Montrose and the two in Dundee.

There are ways they could work together, along the lines I've suggested for clubs in similar circumstances. There's no harm in getting round the table every once in a while and have a brainstorming session. I think this is probably my desired starting point for change. By taking a lead in their respective regions, the football clubs could bring together businesses, councils, schools, etc, and really build a strong infrastructure for the game – set out common aims and objectives, achieve them and then take them out into the wider domain of Scottish football. The regions that are most successful would provide the blueprint for the rest.

Quote of the day – *Arbroath fans: 'We're the best team in Angus!'*

GAME	ARBROATH VERSUS QUEENS PARK
DIVISION	SFL3
DATE	SAT 16 APRIL 2011, KO 3PM
VENUE	GAYFIELD PARK, ATTENDANCE 912
SCORE	2-2

MATCH STATS:
HTTP://WWW.SCOTTISHFOOTBALLLEAGUE.COM/FOOTBALL/THIRD/
RESULTS/3285036/

39

THE BLUE TOON V THE FIFERS

Toon are Doon

I WAS LOOKING FORWARD to the game, but not to the long drive to the northeast and back. Anyway, it had to be done so Google Maps were consulted and approximately five hours was the estimated journey time from Prestwick. Rubbish, I thought. I'd travelled there previously and it was nothing like that long. I set off at about 11am, determined to get this one out of the way. En route, I fired up the SatNav and punched in the postcode. To my horror, the ETA was 3.50. It looked like I would miss the first half! I contemplated turning back and reviewing the rest of fixture list. Could I squeeze in another midweek game? The answer was a resounding no, I had to get to Peterhead today, I just needed some good luck with the traffic. Thankfully, I encountered no problems whatsoever, even going through Aberdeen, and I arrived with half an hour to spare.

This was my first visit to the new stadium. There is a supermarket where the old one used to be – I wonder how many supermarket chains have bought old football grounds in Scotland? There was no problem finding a space in the large car park outside the ground, so I listened to a few more minutes of Radio Scotland. All the talk was about letter bombs and death threats, and yes, it was a football show! What a week it's been. It was all very embarrassing being a football fan in Scotland. We must rise above the madness and get on with enjoying the game we love, and some were getting right into the mood down at East End Park for a big Fife derby, a top of the table clash between Dunfermline and Raith Rovers. The presenters were building the game up, a welcome change from all the nonsense that has dominated their chat for the last few weeks.

My mind returned to the question of whether we'd get more sell-outs if we had more games like the one at East End, ie no Celtic or Rangers – allowing other teams to compete for the prizes. I really

Hollywood entrance

don't know. Thinking back to my visit to see the Pars, the attendance that day was pathetic, especially considering they went top of the league. However, that's another story and argument, today's is about relegation. Peterhead could go down if results go against them. I've never been to a relegation encounter before.

With 20 minutes in hand before kick off, I went for a recce. There are good facilities adjacent to the ground, including artificial pitches and Youth and Community Department playing fields. A football match was under way and I felt this added to the occasion, even though there might not have been a direct link between the club and the youth football. This is the type of thing that should be happening at every ground, youngsters playing in the shadow of the big stadium, aiming one day to play there. I took some pictures and enjoyed the sunshine before heading for the turnstile and parting with my hard-earned cash. It cost £12 to get in, and I felt pleased until I started thinking about how much the seven-hour round trip was costing me – I was looking at an outlay of £50 on fuel.

Inside the stadium I purchased the *Blue Toon Talk* programme (£2), a pie (£2) and Bovril (£1.50), Hovering about beside the railings, I devoured the strange, hybrid pie (half steak, half mince). There was another checkpoint at the stairs to the stand and I decided to go for it, and handed over another £2.

I took a seat near the front and settled down for the afternoon's entertainment. The PA was blasting out classics from a bygone era, more and more fans were arriving via the social club and the teams were out on the park – everything building up nicely for a crucial game for the Blue Toon. The Fifers huddled in the middle of the pitch (which looked a bit like a fairway that had been used by dodgy golfers) and a few shouts could be heard around the place.

The game was pretty even in the early stages and both teams had chances before East Fife gradually took control by playing a sharp, passing game. The visitors took the lead after a good move, looked like an own goal, and never really looked back. Peterhead were a team with no luck, their fate seemed sealed even that early in the game. They were working really hard but nothing was coming off for them and this theme continued up until half-time.

The interval was spent in the usual fashion, reading the programme, scanning the horizon and generally getting a feel for the place. The Blue Toon's programme was reasonably interesting, so much so that I hadn't noticed a torrential downpour! The constant sound of helicopters overhead is hard to miss, as is the big power station that is clearly visible to the south. I decided to use the toilet facilities before the restart and headed down the stairs and into the social club. So this is where the Main Stand supporters all disappeared to – the place was jumping.

In the second half, Peterhead continued to try really hard but still got nowhere. Nothing daunted, their vuvuzela-wielding fans were right behind them, especially the young team who sang virtually from start to finish. East Fife showed no mercy and scored another good goal to seal the points after Peterhead hit the bar – it was one of those days. Another rain shower near the end of the half was the straw that broke the camel's back for many of the Blue Toon Brigade and their season was over a few minutes later when the ref blew for full time.

Peterhead's predicament bewildered me. The stadium was one of the reasons that the club were elected into the SFL from the Highland League. The surrounding area has probably fared better than most during the credit crunch and the competition is hardly at Central Belt proportions. Peterhead's traditional rivals are the Highland League team Fraserburgh. However, since their election to the SFL this rivalry has waned somewhat and they now have a new rivalry with Elgin City. Why then, less than 500 people at this crucial game?

The contrast with what Ross County have achieved is stark. Ross County entered the SFL in 1994, Peterhead in 2000. But while Peterhead will be playing in Division Three, Ross County will be seeking their fortune in the Premier League. Something's not quite right at the Blue

Toon, yet inspiration is only a few miles away in Ross-shire, where Ross County are pulling in an average of upwards of 2,000 per match, probably due to the strong links that the Dingwall club have forged with the local community.

Quote of the day – *Elderly Blue Toon fan: 'Shut that vu vu whatever it is up or I'll shove it up yer arse!'*

GAME	PETERHEAD VERSUS EAST FIFE
DIVISION	SFL2
DATE	SAT 23 APRIL 2011, KO 3PM
VENUE	BALMOOR STADIUM, ATTENDANCE 473
SCORE	0-2

MATCH STATS:
HTTP://WWW.SCOTTISHFOOTBALLLEAGUE.COM/FOOTBALL/SECOND/
RESULTS/3285095/

40

THE BLACK & WHITES V THE BULLY WEE

Clyde in Briggs Triumph

ELGIN WAS THE DESTINATION but given the distance from my home (how on earth do the away fans manage?) I decided to take the week off and take the family up for a few days' holiday. We rented a secluded cabin on the outskirts of town and had a thoroughly enjoyable break. The weather was absolutely scorching the whole time we were there, the location is rather nice – and I went to Borough Briggs for the first time.

I approached the old buildings about ten minutes before kick off. It wasn't exactly Sauchiehall Street but you could tell there was a game on. I continued round past the Main Stand looking for practice pitches and the like. Nothing but greenery and distilleries were to be seen, so I headed towards the turnstile, cash in hand, and emerged into the ground with a big smile on my face: £8 admission – cheapest yet!

My next port of call was the snack bar and as it was too soon after dinner, all I could manage was a Bovril (60p) and a Twix. The programme (£2) was two weeks out of date, but at least they told us, unlike the St Johnstone people. The evening sunshine was disappearing rapidly so I headed up into the Main Stand in the mood to enjoy another Highland football experience.

I chose a seat behind about 30 school children and, while it was good to see the youngsters (and a good number of family groups) in the stadium – they were annoying me. As kick-off time approached the kids got more and more excited and throughout the game their minders were kept busy relaying them to and from the toilet and the snack bar.

But they're the future, I told myself, we've got to make an effort!

Both sides started the game at a high tempo on the lush but bumpy pitch. The players all seemed to be really young, in fact some of the

Welcome to the Briggs

Clyde boys were scrawny as well, certainly not the healthiest looking specimens. The Highlanders looked a bit better, must be all the fresh air. It was end-to-end stuff but all pretty scrappy for most of the first half. The home side had a goal disallowed, much to the annoyance of the youthful support, the tackles were flying in and there were chances at both ends. Elgin's physio was kept busy and generally it was all entertaining enough, even though some of the football was schoolboy level. The half-time score was a dispiriting 0-0.

The programme had very little in it to hold my attention so it was a quick read. With the floodlights on, the stadium looked pretty run-down and brought to mind the infamous Cliftonhill, but the setting was nicer. You get what you pay for, I suppose. The stadium served a purpose, albeit one-dimensional; it was a typical football ground – used once a fortnight. Surely there could be some sort of link to the leisure centre next door? My daydream was disturbed by the 'All Blacks' (the stewards' uniforms were black and they looked like bouncers), who seemed to be constantly coming and going to the hospitality area behind me, often carrying money in tins. This is something that I've come across often on my travels through the lower leagues – money in tins and Tupperware containers, not a debit card in sight!

Teams out for the second half and there were chances for both sides with the Clyde goalie pulling off a great save. Seven minutes from time the visitors scored a winning goal. Elgin responded by tackling even harder and giving their all but no equaliser materialised and the game finished 1-0 to the Lanarkshire side.

I was back in our holiday cabin, beer in hand, within ten minutes, having enjoyed my visit to Borough Briggs. The smaller teams really appeal to me. Unfortunately, Elgin 'City' would appear to appeal rather less to the good people of Elgin – only 272 were in attendance on a lovely spring night. And yet I'm convinced it's within the club's power to attract more punters.

The lack of numbers at the game might have been down to various reasons, including too many games over the season, repetitiveness and no visiting fans. But can supporters really be expected to travel up to Elgin from Glasgow on a Tuesday night? No chance – it must be hard enough getting the players and club staff away up here midweek.

Like many other clubs, Elgin have strong foundations in the local community primarily through Elgin City FC Community Football. These initiatives take time to bear fruit but the more we have, the more chance we have of improving the game in Scotland. And as mentioed earlier, Youth Football Scotland can give guidance on everything a youth club needs to set up and operate. I'm surprised that the governing bodies don't offer a similar type of one-stop shop facility for senior football clubs.

All in all it was an interesting evening and good to see a trend developing in terms of grassroots football – if only we could sort out the big boys!

Quote of the day – *Teacher to lively youths: 'Will you stop making so much noise!' Is that not what it's all about?*

GAME	ELGIN CITY VERSUS CLYDE
DIVISION	SFL3
DATE	TUE 26 APRIL 2011, KO 7.45PM
VENUE	BOROUGH BRIGGS, ATTENDANCE 272
SCORE 0-1	

MATCH STATS:
HTTP://WWW.SCOTTISHFOOTBALLLEAGUE.COM/FOOTBALL/THIRD/
RESULTS/3379031/

THE ROVERS V THE DOONHAMERS

Hammer Blow at the San Starko

TIME TO TAKE in today's action in Kirkcaldy – Raith Rovers v Queen of the South. I decided to join the Doonhamers faithful in the North Stand for the afternoon's proceedings and in the throng (not kidding) outside Stark's Park. I tried in vain to purchase a programme and was dismayed to learn that they were sold out, which messed up my set for this once-in-a-lifetime journey through Scottish football. I bit the bullet and, £16 lighter, I was inside the San Starko for the first time and looking for the snack bar. Nightmare! No steak pies, so the dreaded Scotch pie was purchased along with a Bovril (£1.60 each) and it was straight on up into the stand on an absolutely beautiful day for a game. The pitch was bathed in sunshine and the views over the town and out to sea were fabulous – this place could be a contender for best football view in Scotland. My pie was OK, as was the Bovril.

I looked around at all the empty seats. Outside, it had felt as if there was going to be a massive crowd, yet the place was nowhere near full. Pratt Street seemed to be the only way in and out as the other side of Stark's Park is bordered by a railway line, and so all the supporters were funnelled to one side of the ground, making it feel busier than it really was.

The small crowd made a bit of noise as the game kicked off and both sides went about their business in a sprightly fashion. Raith were still in with a chance of promotion, albeit results had to go their way over the last few games and that would be almost impossible, but it could still make for a good game. I hadn't seen them since a Scottish Cup tie at Alloa, which they surprisingly lost, so I didn't really know what to expect from them. As for the Doonhamers, I had seen them

A real fitba' stand

home and away to Dunfermline, one win one loss, which pretty much summed up their season.

The game rumbled on with Raith generally in control and Queens counter-attacking when they could. There were chances for both sides, off the post and crossbar, and some reasonable football on the deck as well. The stadium remained pretty quiet and was almost silenced when the news filtered through that Dunfermline had scored at Morton – the season was over for the Kirkcaldy side. Both teams continued to have a go but I felt they lacked real conviction and this was annoying as I had Raith on my coupon. The score was 0-0 at the break.

I tried once more to get my hands on a programme but to no avail, all I managed to find was the smoking area. Disappointed, I headed back up into the stand. At least you could watch the trains going by.

I had imagined that Stark's Park was a fully redeveloped modern stadium due to the cantilevered steelwork that supports the roofs on the north and south stands. Not so. The old Main Stand sits askew in one corner, a remnant of yesteryear. It reminded me of a cricket clubhouse (as it may well have been in a previous life) and, to an extent, of the Main Stand at Dens Park. Another remnant of yesteryear was the football rattle that one of the Queens' fans had. I remembered this from my trip to Palmerston earlier in the season – probably it was the same person.

It was breezy in the shade and I noticed that a few people were

Glorious in Raith

moving down towards the sunny section, but an over officious steward, determined to maintain a ticker-tape segregation line, was turning them back. Second half under way, the action on the pitch was hotting up, handbags were being thrown about and the crowd were finally roused. There wasn't much between the teams, Raith were huffing and puffing, Queens were happy to sit back and hit on the break and looking more likely to score. I was getting nervous. And yes, it happened again: a goal against the run of play. I've seen so many games like this, it makes me wonder why I gamble. The goal basically ended the contest and the remaining minutes were played out at a much lower tempo, both teams willing the ref to blow for full time, which he duly did, bringing my First Division experience to a close for the season.

It was a disappointing end to what had promised to be an exciting season for Raith (the only team that had let me down, so a reasonable day at the bookies was had). I began analysing the Kirkcaldy team. Could Raith make a meaningful contribution to an extended Premier League? Possibly, but certainly not on today's attendance figures. Like so many clubs in Scotland they should be in a better position and I wonder if they have done everything possible to improve their position.

Back in the '6os, during Scottish football's heyday, would Stark's Park have been bulging at the seams and Raith challenging for trophies? Was the league actually better and more competitive in those days? The history books confirm it was, with Celtic, Dundee, Hearts,

Kilmarnock and Rangers all winning the top division in the swinging decade. Raith peaked in 1967, making it into the top division after finishing runners-up in the 20-strong Division Two. Previously, in 1921, they were responsible for an innovation previously unknown to the Scottish game: following a visit to England, the Raith directors introduced the use of a ball in training. As noted in the *Fife Free Press*: 'Hitherto, ball practice has been an absentee from the training curriculum on the grounds that being away from the ball for a week imparted eagerness on the Saturday.' This heralded an era of success.

Raith also tasted success in season 1994/95 with a First Division title and a remarkable penalty shoot-out victory against Celtic in the League Cup Final. These achievements may stir warm memories for the club's fans, but they are too few and far between and simply serve to underline the fact that the structure of Scottish football must be altered to give the smaller clubs a better shot at the big prizes.

If I lived in Kirkcaldy I would go and watch Raith, I'd see it as a great way to spend an afternoon with friends and family. So why don't more people go? This is the question that the myriad authorities should be asking – not 'How can we get more TV money?', a question that is never going to trigger the rebirth of Scottish football.

Quote of the day – Doonhamers faithful singing: 'You're gonnae win f**k all!'

GAME	RAITH ROVERS VERSUS QUEEN OF THE SOUTH
DIVISION	SFL1
DATE	SAT 30 APRIL 2011, KO 3PM
VENUE	STARK'S PARK, ATTENDANCE 2,001
SCORE	0-1

MATCH STATS:
HTTP://WWW.SCOTTISHFOOTBALLLEAGUE.COM/FOOTBALL/FIRST/
RESULTS/3285187/

42

THE TIC V THE ARABS

Spring Encounter, Very Few Arabs

HARD ON THE HEELS of my trip to the San Starko, the Sunday match was a trip to Celtic Park, home of the 'other half' of Glasgow. Parkhead has never been one of my favourite places, for obvious reasons, but also because as a youngster I was often left in the car on Westmuir Street while my dad went for a couple of pints in one of the infamous hostelries, leaving me to put up with Celtic supporters banging on the windows and roof, having a laugh to themselves. No harm ever came to me but the memories linger and the area is not one of my favourites even though I'm an East End boy. As a supporter of Rangers, Celtic Park was never the happiest of hunting grounds either, and throw in that infamous Scotland match when Gary McAllister was booed (I booed – I'm totally embarrassed by that now), most of my associations with the place are far from positive. Never mind, Parkhead here I come – just hope nobody sees me!

Two years had passed since my last time here, for the Champions League qualifier against Arsenal. My brother-in-law supports the English Premier side and we went along early in the ill-fated Tony Mowbray era. Arsenal won at a canter with the gulf in class clear to see, a sobering reminder of where Scottish football is in the great scheme of things. Anyway, times and personnel have changed significantly at Celtic since then, so much so that this is a crucial match in the championship race, with the Old Firm neck-and-neck as the season draws to a close.

Better get a move on – game on at Parkhead in an hour and I was still in Prestwick. The nearer the venue, the later you leave. I had a plan though: the better half would drop me off just before kick off and come back and pick me up, which would save all that parking palaver. In theory it would be quieter as nearly everyone would be inside.

Commemorating Celtic's most famous team

I got out on London Road and I headed into Celtic Park on a match day. With my £25 ticket in hand, I ran through the other latecomers up Kinloch Street to the entrance about five minutes after the 12.45 kick off. I let myself in via the electronic turnstile and climbed the stairs at the southeast corner.

The game was in full flow and I sat down at the end of Row K. Some adjustments to the seating arrangements were required though, as my seat was occupied due to the adjacent one being broken. All settled, it was good to be back at a 'big game' with fast football in a good stadium. My view was excellent – I had requested the unrestricted view section when purchasing my ticket via telephone from the Dundee United ticket office. The atmosphere was good too, so there were all the ingredients for a great game of football.

Much as I had enjoyed my saunter through the lower leagues, you can't beat the top division, the whole set-up is just so much more professional. Celtic were already in control and looking to take an early lead. United were stubborn in defence in the opening stages but occasionally looked a bit wobbly as the game wore on. Both sets of fans were getting behind their teams with the home support obviously louder than their counterparts from the City of Discovery. Inevitably, Celtic scored the goal halfway through the first period and never really looked to be in any serious trouble. This was a wee bit disappointing as the Tangerines were in good form and I was expecting a better showing. They did break on a few occasions but their performance was lacklustre throughout. Half time, 1-0 to the Glasgow side.

Like the day before at Stark's Park, the break was spent without a programme – this was getting really annoying. Due to my late arrival I hadn't managed to get one on the way in, so I ventured down into the bowels of the stand and asked one of the hi-viz brigade if he knew where I could purchase one. All I got was a vacant look. I decided my best bet would be after the game (and I did get one a few days later, online). I wasn't hungry after my late breakfast so at the snack bar I limited myself to crisps and a drink – around £3 for the two items, premier prices. I had to laugh at the sign beside the kiosk – 'We don't accept £50 notes' – there was a certain irony there. The snack bar itself was pretty dismal for a stadium like Celtic Park, and the menu was basic to say the least. As I started down the stairs, I stopped and took in the entire Dundee United support. There could only have been a couple of hundred at most.

Back on the park there was a presentation for the under-19s who had won the league. What a feeling there was for those boys out there, virtually the whole stadium was cheering for them. What a motivator that might prove to be for their future careers – good stuff.

Dundee United seemed a bit more purposeful after the break, which was good for all concerned. The atmosphere remained positive as well, particularly the mob high up in the corner, who sang and cheered throughout. It was at this point that I noticed how many empty seats there were around the stadium. This was worrying, to say the least, not unlike the situation at Ibrox a few weeks before. I just wish the clubs would remember times are tough at the moment, and not just with the admission prices.

Celtic scored again and there was no way back for United. They huffed and puffed but there was nothing forthcoming from either side and as the clock ticked towards 85 minutes I decided to make my exit. Now I hate leaving games early, but the better half was driving and considering her unfamiliarity with the area and football traffic I had told her I would be out sharp, and duly made my exit – the rest, as they say, is history.

I ran back to my drop-off point, was picked up within minutes –

Great day for the young bhoys

I love it when a plan comes together – and we drove to my dad's house. He enquired about the score: 2-0 was my reply, completely oblivious of the fact that I had missed three goals in my rush to get out!

And Celtic, well, what is left to say about them. A huge club in a small league in a small country. I fully understood the weight of this now, having visited all but two of the senior grounds. It really sinks in when you see the rest of the chasing pack. The departure of Rangers and Celtic would significantly level the playing field, but how would Scottish football fare without them? That's the million dollar question.

Of course recent events at Rangers have changed things significantly. Celtic insist that their wellbeing is immaterial to the situation at Rangers. Many other clubs in the league feel that a weakened Rangers will even things up a little and are seizing the moment to have a go at changing the voting structure in the top league. But would a league without or with a weakened Rangers increase competition, or would it just further strengthen Celtic's position at the top? I feel that the latter would be the case.

And one last thought, on the sectarianism that continues to blight the Old Firm. If Celtic and Rangers were to leave Scottish football and play in a more competitive league, would the focus move away from religion and onto football? If the fans were anticipating upcoming big games against Chelsea or Arsenal or Manchester United or the like, would they still have the inclination to bicker about their rivals on the other side of the city? Would the goldfish bowl mentality disappear as new rivalries develop? Would the madness that envelopes Old Firm days in Scotland fade? And would we need the Scottish Parliament to pass laws on how to behave in football stadiums? I take the view that Celtic and Rangers leaving the Scottish Premier League could be beneficial not only to football but to society in general.

Quote of the day – *Me: 'Where are all the Dundee United fans?'*

GAME	CELTIC VERSUS DUNDEE UNITED
DIVISION	SPL
DATE	SUN I MAY 2011, KO 12.45PM
VENUE	CELTIC PARK, ATTENDANCE 48,599
SCORE	4-1

MATCH STATS:
HTTP://WWW.SCOTPREM.COM/CONTENT/DEFAULT.ASP?PAGE=S9_1_1&
WORKINGDATE=2011-5-1

43

THE DONS V THE SAINTS

Sheepish Performance from the Dons

THE LAST SATURDAY fixture of the season – destination Aberdeen. I parked on the esplanade and paused to enjoy the views out over the North Sea, and watch the support vessels from the oil industry in a kind of watery no man's land between the harbour and the open sea. It was warm and hazy and the whole area was busy with people doing all sorts of leisure activities; walking, running, practising golf... I sat and listened to the radio for a while, more Old Firm talk, this time about Rangers – the club had just been sold for £1. Then I set off across the golf course, dodging the balls from the driving range – incredibly, some were getting over the fence – I hoped the footballers would be a bit better!

I arrived at the back of the Richard Donald Stand and was quite impressed by the look of the stadium and the activity all around the place. This was however short-lived – first impressions can sometimes be misleading. Pittodrie Stadium had changed little in the 20-odd years since my last visit.

I wandered around outside the Main Stand, checked out the club shop and, crucially, bought my programme at the first opportunity – last weekend's mistakes would not be repeated. One of the hi-viz brigade pointed me in the direction of the visiting supporters' section. There was no way a Glaswegian would get away with sitting among the Dons faithful, so I would be a Saint for the day. The route to the South Stand took me through a few car parks, all very well secured with steel palisade fencing, and past some newish looking flats, all very regimented, I thought. This part of the stadium was pretty quiet, in fact there were only a handful of fans heading for the turnstiles.

I parted with the £22 admission fee and carried on through. On further inspection, I realised that the ticket was one that could have been used in an electronic turnstile. It's good that they have facilities like this available but strange that they don't use them to the full potential.

First stop was the toilets, which were portacabins downstairs and a more traditional offering upstairs, both clean and functional but I'd expected a bit more from a club of Aberdeen's stature. I was whingeing like an Aberdonian – stop complaining and get to the snack bar, I said to myself. If the prices were anything like last week at Celtic Park, this could be an expensive meal. Fortunately, they weren't. A good steak pie and a delicious Bovril were purchased for £2 and £1.60 respectively, hardly Premier prices. I hung about at the top of the stand enjoying my food and the glorious views – yet another contender for best view in Scotland.

As kick-off time approached, I selected an end-of-row seat. It was in pretty poor condition, just like the rest of them. I was sure that Pittodrie used to claim to be the first all-seated stadium in Britain, it's time they replaced the originals.

As the teams emerged the decibel level rose slightly but all the excitement was put on hold for an impeccable minute's silence for Eddie Turnbull who had recently passed away. The game started slowly and got slower, two teams with nothing but pride to play for slogging it out at the end of a long season. This is was the third time I'd seen Aberdeen (twice before under Craig Brown and once under Mark McGhee), and again they were terrible. They completely lacked conviction and this transfers to the stands where the home crowd did little to urge their team on.

As I've said, Scottish football needs a strong Aberdeen. Have the power brokers at Pittodrie not realised this? Surely we can expect bet-

Thanks for the memories

ter from this proud football club? Well, not today. St Johnstone took the lead early in the first half with what looked like an own goal and remained comfortable throughout. They moved the ball around well, were purposeful going forward and were first to the 50-50 challenges

Will the Red Army rise again?

when required. Aberdeen's resurgence in form during the early days of Craig Brown's era was a distant memory. They offered little during a dull first half. Hopefully, the second would be better. Half-time - 1-0 to the visitors.

At last something positive – I spent the entire break reading the excellent match day magazine – *Red*. This was arguably the best £3 I've spent all season. The magazine covered three different matches, all over a period of ten days, and so the content remained in context. *Red* offers a comprehensive look at the football club, past and present (and yes, they did mention Gothenburg), and other interesting features. This is the type of magazine you would want to buy every other week, it's great template for other clubs – Scottish football take note! I was so engrossed that I'd failed to notice that the rain was starting to come in off the North Sea, so I took refuge higher up in the stand for the second half, which was just about to kick off.

After a slight delay the game recommenced and the Dons came out all guns blazing. Unfortunately, they were firing blanks, mostly over the roof of the stand, and the Saints quickly regained control. This wouldn't be a game of two halves. My view was slightly better now as the slope was less evident – Pittodrie seems to be slipping towards the sea! The visitors eventually doubled their lead and it was effectively game over. The exodus of Dons faithful started at about 4.25. I was more interested in the helicopters flying overhead. The same couldn't be said of the Perth supporters, they sang and cheered their team on throughout, although the 'banter' aimed at Jamie Langfield's wife was very distasteful.

I was home just after 8. It had been a long day, no doubt about that, but enjoyable all the same. As usual I spent the journey reflecting on the day's events. I came to the conclusion that Aberdeen, one of Scotland's biggest clubs, were in need of major surgery. What hope do the rest of them have when a club based in such an affluent city are in such a poor state? This club should be challenging for the league title every year; if they're not, then they're only making up the numbers – and that is exactly what is happening. Too many clubs in the Premier League are doing no more than fulfilling their fixtures and this must change, the sooner the better.

As for the stadium, years of neglect had taken their toll and the place needed a major refurbishment. Expecting fans to turn up week after week to this crumbling arena is an overly nonchalant approach that will result in less and less paying punters. Surely it makes sound business sense for the club to invest in one of their primary assets.

The good news is that there is recent, positive news on the stadium Planning permission has been granted for its redevelopment and several offers for Pittodrie, which is crucial to the deal, have been received. The new development will be more than just a football stadium. It is described as a community facility with indoor and outdoor pitches, sports hall, gymnasium, two fitness suites, changing rooms, meeting room, cafe and offices. Aberdeen vice-convener John Corall announced: 'This is a welcome addition to the city. It will be of enormous benefit to not just the professional and amateur football players, but it will also have significant social and sports benefits for the wider community.'

It all makes me think how very few businesses have the lifelong loyal customers that football clubs have. Some clever individual must take on board all these plus points and deliver a business model that will help Scottish clubs to grow and prosper.

The new Aberdeen stadium is a step in the right direction – next up, the football team.

Quote of the day – *Saints fan: 'I would hate tae be a sheep the night after that performance!'*

GAME	ABERDEEN VERSUS ST JOHNSTONE
DIVISION	SPL
DATE	SAT 7 MAY 2011, KO 3PM
VENUE	PITTODRIE STADIUM, ATTENDANCE 6,361
SCORE	0-2

MATCH STATS:
HTTP://WWW.SCOTPREM.COM/CONTENT/DEFAULT.ASP?PAGE=S1_1_1&
WORKINGDATE=2011-5-7

44

CALEY THISTLE V THE HIBEES

No Highland Fling for Hibs

I'VE REACHED THE final game in my personal crusade through Scottish football. OK, crusade is probably too strong a word, tour is more like it. Anyway, tonight's match in Inverness is the last – the end is nigh.

As it was midweek, I'd booked into a Travelodge on the outskirts of Inverness, planning to leave early in the morning and get to work on schedule. I managed a quick bite to eat in the restaurant next to my digs and then drove to the Tulloch Caledonian Stadium. As usual, my chosen radio programme was focusing on the Old Firm with Celtic's trip to Tynecastle the main feature. Walter Smith's last home game at Ibrox the previous evening was also on the agenda as the title race excitement reached fever pitch. Unbeknown to the commentators, the events that were about to unfold at Tynecastle would fill every column inch and every airwave for days to come.

With the iPhone in camera mode, I strolled towards the stadium taking pictures and enjoying the atmosphere. I noticed a few youngsters walking around with empty boxes and immediately started to panic, worrying that the programmes had sold out already but I located another vendor behind the North Stand and got my hands on the very last one. Relieved, I headed for the turnstile and entered my last, but not least, senior Scottish ground; £21 got me in. A ticket was presented with my change and I was pleased about that, I'm always keen on memorabilia. The caravan type food outlet behind the West Stand had a reasonable selection of food and drink but as I'd already eaten a chocolate bar sufficed.

The stand somehow seemed like a temporary structure, but it was comfortable enough and offered good views of the surrounding area. Teams out – game on in Inverness!

The two sides started brightly. It was a perfect evening for football and the pitch looked fine. There were all the ingredients for a good game, except for the atmosphere, which was virtually non-existent. This was the quietest ground yet.

The away side were playing the better football – this was generally the case with Hibs on the four occasions I'd seen them this season. They did have an off day against Ayr United at Easter Road in the cup but they have always tried to play good passing football and tonight was no exception. The majority of the chances were falling to the visiting team, a goal looked inevitable and it came after 40 minutes. You guessed – Inverness took the lead. Another game another goal totally against the run of play – I'm never betting again! At half time it was 1-0 to ICT.

The programme was both entertaining and interesting, particularly Big Terry's thoughts on restructuring which are similar to my own. A top division of 14 (I agree) with a six-team split for European places and an eight team spilt for relegation – I would go for seven and seven. He also comments on amalgamating the SPL with the SFL and restructuring the SFA and is keen on a winter break. Supporters Direct Scotland backs similar changes, based on surveys carried out amongst fans; nine out of ten want bigger league set-ups, a clear majority want a shift to 'summer' football – March to November, two-thirds stated that they would attend more often if there was more competition and most wanted supporter representation on club boards and with the authorities. Clearly there is an appetite for change – when is it going to happen?

Anyway back to the game. Hibs continued to push and ICT was doing the defending. The pace had dropped a bit, which was understandable; as at Pittodrie last Saturday, the teams were only playing for pride. However, Inverness soon doubled their lead with a goal of the season contender and took control of proceedings thereafter. Hibs were now a beaten team and nothing was coming off for them. They still tried to play football but so did Inverness and the game was competitive and good to watch till the end. The crowd were pretty quiet throughout and that included the handful of Hibs fans that had made the journey north.

And then it was all over. The ref blew for full time in Inverness and in so doing signalled me getting my life back – or so I thought!

I slowly made my way to the car, contemplating what I had achieved. A lifelong ambition to visit all the grounds had been achieved, and in one season – time for a celebratory pint. I was in the boozer within 15

Only one Big Mac in Inverness

minutes, pint in hand and a satisfied smile on my face.

Inverness Caledonian Thistle were still firmly in my thoughts, but I decided to have another few beers, the game review can wait one more night!

Inverness, with a population of well over 50,000 and one of Scotland's fastest growing cities, has an interesting football club. Formed in 1994 after the merger of Caledonian and Inverness Thistle, ICT have steadily made their way from the Third Division to the Scottish Premier with a few notable results along the way. The club are now established in the higher echelons of football in Scotland and will soon be joined in the top flight with their neighbours, Ross County, who have followed a similar path. Another thing these clubs have in common is the close links they have made with their local communities and this has been a key factor in their successes. Both recognise this and continue to engage locally through youth development, shared facilities and other initiatives, that are coming to fruition for the Highlanders. Other clubs beware, there could be an uprising!

Despite all this, I think that the crowd of 3,344 was pretty poor, particularly in light of recent achievements and the infrastructure that's in place. I wondered how the city was faring in the post-boom period – a few years back everyone and their granny seemed to heading up here to live. Hopefully, some of the incomers would come along and support the team with the locals but that maybe wasn't the case.

OK, I know it was the end of the season, but I had honestly expected more people here. Or is football just not as popular in the Highlands? I understood the travel difficulties that both the home and travelling fans would face, particularly in the winter, as the A9 and A96 are not the best roads in the country – another point in favour of Marvember football.

Change is in the air and I've now seen and written enough to understand Scottish football a wee bit better. Time to set down my thoughts on the way ahead for Scottish football.

Quote of the day – *Me: 'Well done.'*

GAME	ICT VERSUS HIBERNIAN
DIVISION	SPL
DATE	WED 11TH MAY 2011, KO 7.45PM
VENUE	TC STADIUM, ATTENDANCE 3,344
SCORE	2-0

MATCH STATS:
HTTP://WWW.SCOTPREM.COM/CONTENT/DEFAULT.ASP?PAGE=S25_1_1
&WORKINGDATE=2011-5-11

The Way Ahead?

IT'S NEVER BEEN MORE IMPORTANT for the focus to be on what matters – the state of Scottish football, and what can be done to improve the game. Not everyone will share my opinions on the way ahead, but I hope that the arguments presented below will open up the constructive debate we need and bring the fans centre stage.

A Different League Set-Up?

LEAGUE RECONSTRUCTION

League reconstruction has to be implemented, but only after careful consideration. There has been much debate and this should be allowed to continue until a reasonable consensus is reached. The final outcome will not please everyone – that goes without saying.

Nevertheless something has to happen, and happen soon – the fans are fed up with the same teams playing each other at least four times a season. All stakeholders need to get round the table and agree on the best way forward.

The BBC reported on 16 April 2012 that the Scottish FA is considering setting up a National Football League to replace the Scottish Premier League and the Scottish Football League. A senior SFL source expressed cautious optimism:

> This could come about if the people running the SPL and the SFL don't get their act together There are clubs almost dying all round the country while nothing happens.

And an SFA source commented:

> It would almost be a benevolent act to bring the two warring factions together for the good of Scottish football.

These quotes underline the urgency of the present situation and underline how seriously the deep divisions within Scottish football are hampering progress.

TWO POTENTIAL STRUCTURES

Like Terry Butcher, I favour the 14-team, three-league set-up with a top–bottom split. After 26 league matches, the top seven teams in the new Premier Division would play off for the European places (if we still have any) and the bottom seven would fight the relegation battle. There would only be six matches after the split, resulting in a total of 32 league games – plenty, in my opinion. The Premier and First Divisions would be set up similarly (obviously, the First wouldn't have the European places available in the Premier Division).

The Second Division relegation issue would also need to be considered, ie who could come up.

Supporters Direct Scotland favours two leagues of 16 playing each other twice, with a qualifying league of ten playing each other four times, making up 42 places. In their proposed model, promotion and relegation arrangements are a combination of automatic and play-off places through the three leagues. sds claim that this is one way of increasing competition as recommended in the official review, where Henry McLeish recommends:

> There should be more competition within our professional game. This should be achieved by more promotion and relegation and play-offs between competing leagues. This will provide more interest and more incentive.

In either case, the benefits are appealing: more variety than the current set-up, fewer games overall, fewer meaningless mid-table games, fewer midweek games, higher level of anticipation for seeing other teams and, crucially, more space for younger players to develop.

I know that many club directors may have sleepless nights at the thought of fewer games but there is an old saying: 'Less is more.' Football can become monotonous and very costly when teams are playing Saturday, Tuesday, Saturday, Wednesday, etc. Fewer scheduled matches taken as a whole would be more affordable for supporters, hence attendances would be likely to increase. Also, less repetition in terms of team pairing would whet the fans' appetite for games.

I fully understand the importance of tv money for the clubs, but at the moment we are at saturation point – there is quite simply too much football on television. It's time the relevant authorities listened to the fans, who are in favour of larger leagues rather than structuring the leagues to suit TV. Empty stadiums broadcast around Britain and beyond are an embarrassment. So let's extend the leagues, televise less football and get more fans through those turnstiles – I think it's a winner.

SHOULD THE OLD FIRM DEPART THE SCOTTISH PREMIER LEAGUE?

It's only when you see the chasing pack that you realise just how big Rangers and Celtic are within the Scottish leagues. They really are in a class of their own and they need a fresh challenge – but where should they go? There's been talk of forming a North Atlantic League but that's not their preferred option.

Both clubs have mentioned an interest in moving to the English Premier League, but the reception to that idea from down south has been lukewarm. Here's a possible way to break down that resistance.

Celtic, Rangers and the Old Firm can be seen as three separate brands, all operating on a global level, albeit not quite as high profile as the likes of Manchester United and Chelsea. Their strong appeal the world over has to be used more effectively.

The Old Firm brand is the big one. A strategy for building interest in it overseas must be developed as a joint effort between Rangers and Celtic. Once the Old Firm brand establishes a better foothold in the global market, Rangers and Celtic as individual brands should then be further developed.

It's blatantly obvious to me that not only the TV companies but also the English Premier League would be champing at the bit for some of the action and I'm surprised that this type of thing has not been mooted before.

So how would Scottish football fare without the big two? Well, hopefully they wouldn't leave altogether. My preference would be that Rangers and Celtic would still have a presence and would participate in the Scottish and League Cups. They could even have reserve teams playing in Scotland. And of course, they would still be based here.

The chasing pack stand to benefit from any arrangement that loosens the stranglehold the big two currently have on the game in this country. Everyone will prosper. All Scottish fans would be excited to see at least half a dozen teams competing for the SPL title and with more chance of getting involved in European football. It all makes complete sense.

Yes, I did have my doubts about the smaller teams raising the bar after my trip to East End Park when only a paltry crowd mustered to see Dunfermline take top spot in the First Division, but the approach of Christmas could explain the poor turnout (and the attendances towards the end of season 2010/11 at Dunfermline were encouraging).

Any Old Firm move out of the SPL is no doubt a long way off but I think it will eventually happen. In the meantime, the smaller clubs will continue to make up the numbers with no realistic chance of winning the Premier League and little chance of European football – it's so disheartening for the supporters.

The Old Firm dominance argument is perfectly summed up by this season's Scottish Cup Final – Hearts v Hibs at Hampden on 19 May 2012, a hugely important event for the fans. Hearts legend John Roberston summed it up: 'For one set of fans it will be the greatest day of their lives. For the losers, it will be the toughest of results to take.'

For me, the biggest winner will be Scottish football because, believe it or not, this will be the first time the two clubs have met in the Cup Final since 1896.

The people of Edinburgh, former players of the respective clubs and the fans are all thrilled at the prospect, but why has it taken so long for the Edinburgh clubs to get this chance? I would say that the problem, certainly over the last 12 years, has been down to the Old Firm dominating proceedings, although the two Glasgow giants can't really be held responsible for the limited success of their Edinburgh neighbours in this competition. However, it's clear to me that if Hearts and Hibs were regularly competing to win the league, then they would have more chance of success in this tournament as well.

Given that I'm discussing the possibility of a strong Rangers and Celtic leaving the SPL, the implications of the Rangers crisis demand to be addressed. However, at time of writing, exiting administration remains the club's primary goal and the situation is extremely fluid, with disturbing rumours emerging about Rangers' finances, potential bidders etc.

There are just too many unanswered questions about Rangers' plight to come to any definite conclusions at this point. The imposition by the SFA of a £160,000 fine and a 12-month ban on signing players aged over 18 was met with dismay by the Rangers Supporters Trust who described it as 'a shameful decision'. With every day bringing new developments, the only certainty is that the club will be weaker in the foreseeable future – and that's a sad situation for Scottish football.

Here I'll also touch briefly on the issue of sectarianism. The Scottish Government has brought in new laws to stamp it out but so far it has proved impossible to eradicate.

Does the tenacity of this problem have something to do with the fact there is little or no sustained competition from anywhere else for the big two? Healthy rivalry is one thing, but the pressure resulting from this two-horse race undoubtedly ratchets up the tension. (I notice that a parallel situation has developed recently in Spain's La Liga, where Barcelona and Real Madrid dominate – is Spain now experiencing the Glasgow 'goldfish bowl' effect?)

REGIONAL LEAGUES

Regional leagues are worth considering as a possibility, particularly for the lower divisions. The league format could start with a regional group with the winners/top two going into the main division proper. I think this would benefit many of the part-time clubs as travelling to some away games, especially midweek, is a real burden.

A local set-up would ensure less travelling and possibly more participation from, for example, junior clubs and SDS are in favour of this type of set up both for entry into the lowest tier of the senior leagues and for the League Cup. These mini-league formats were used previously for the League Cup and would be structured geographically for the initial rounds.

I feel that this makes more sense than travelling all over the country all season and would hopefully open the door for younger players, particularly in the latter stages of the groups when further qualification is not possible. Henry McLeish recommends this type of pyramid set-up as it inextricably links all levels of football, from elite to grass roots, and UEFA also recommend this system.

FRIDAY NIGHT FOOTBALL

I'm definitely in favour of Friday night football, but keep it local. It would be great to start the weekend with a game of football and then a few beers, leaving the rest of the weekend free. To me, it's a mystery as to why we don't use this night of the week for football, especially considering how many organisations now finish early on Friday afternoons.

Yes, I know there may be policing issues, but these can be overcome. All credit to the SPL and the SFL for giving the go-ahead to some Friday night fixtures during season 2011/12. The reaction has generally been favourable, particularly when the fans don't have too far to travel – keep it local and it will provide another option.

The now crucial 2014 World Cup qualifying campaign will also see a couple of Friday night fixtures. Craig Levein and his troops will entertain Wales and Macedonia with evening kick-offs. While this may not suit the Tartan Army legions that travel from further afield, the manager seems happy with the fixture list.

We must be united in our efforts to get back onto the main footballing stage.

MORE PLAY-OFFS

Just look at how successful the Championship play-offs in England are every year – they provide incredible excitement for the fans. They're too nerve-wracking for some, but I say bring it on – it's great entertainment. The lower divisions in Scotland have introduced play-offs recently and they have been a success. Any opportunities to have a play-off should be grasped – they keep things interesting to the very end of the season for more people – a definite winner.

- ✓ fans will be at the heart of league reconstruction
- ✓ league reconstruction could dispel Old Firm dominance
- ✓ reconstruction will provide more variety and competition
- ✓ a change will reinvigorate the interests of the fans
- ✓ regional leagues can open the door for younger players
- ✓ Friday night football and play-offs hold wide appeal

The Scottish Football Season

CHANGE TO A MARCH TO NOVEMBER SEASON

The idea of changing the football season calendar is gathering support. For example, SFA President Campbell Ogilvie recently told the BBC:

> From somebody who always said football must be played from August through to May, I am starting to take a different view of the matter.

Scottish women's and girls' football already has a March to November calendar, and Sheila Begbie, SFA Women's Football Co-ordinator, is convinced of the benefits. She says:

> The rise of the Scotland women's national team and the success of Glasgow City in reaching the last 16 of the Champions League were made possible by the change, with players getting the chance to play more often in weather and surfaces conducive to good football.

Personally, I have always been reluctant to go to football when the weather is good enough for gardening or a day at the beach. Winter 2010/11 was exceptionally bad but even on the best winter days there is much to be debated about spectator sports outdoors. Cold weather not only detracts from the individual spectator's experience, it impacts on the quality of the football, and there are potential safety and time issues for travel to and from games.

So it's Marvember for me. The more I researched and thought about it, the more sense it made. The games I watched when the weather was good were quite simply better. Now I know that even during spring, summer and autumn the weather in Scotland can be appalling, but we have to do everything possible to improve the game and shifting the season to the months with better weather would eliminate one of the most significant detrimental factors. Do you think that Barcelona would be as good if they played in these conditions? I doubt it!

A Marvember season would be more comfortable for the supporters and make it safer getting to and from grounds. It's simply more appealing to go and watch a game when the weather's good rather than trudging along to a ground in freezing conditions in the dark. (December 3 2010 will forever be etched in the minds of the many people who were stuck in their cars overnight when the transport network shut down, due to the weather, right in the middle of the football season.)

The football would improve because the pitches and conditions would be better. The players would have less need to worry about frozen pitches and the injuries that they can cause. The change might also improve Scotland's dreadful track record for European qualifying campaigns because the clubs would be at full speed for the July/August start. Players from the English and other leagues could possibly use the different schedule to get fit or get match practice (the transfer windows would need to be altered, there are definite possibilities here).

Some might ask, would Sky Sports and other major sports broadcasters be interested in covering summer games? I would anticipate no problem here. They would see that it could be very lucrative, particularly because there's often very little of significance competing for viewer attention. Lining up against a Marvember season are traditionalists, sticklers for rules and regulations, and those who would point to the competition from other summer holiday activities.

As far as I can see, the biggest issue is culture shock. It's worth noting that Rugby League made the change in the mid-'90s and has never looked back. A new elite league, the Super League, was formed, the sport switched from a winter to a summer season and the value of its TV contract and top tier game crowd attendances have both grown ever since.

If we are serious about improving the game, a switchover to a Marvember season should be at the top of the agenda. How many other sports choose the most inappropriate season to play important games? How many other events are scheduled for outdoors in winter when they could be held at other periods throughout the year? I'm now converted and am fully behind the Marvember season, the sooner the better.

✓ proportionately more good weather March–November
✓ good weather conducive to better quality play
✓ supporter experience enhanced
✓ dangerous travelling conditions less likely
✓ less player injury

Kick-off Times

EARLY WEEKEND KICK-OFFS

Is 3pm still the best kick-off time the majority of our matches? I don't think it is. Yes, lots of matches are kicking off at different times nowadays, and many fans are up in arms about it. However, I am convinced that the 3pm weekend kick-off needs to be reviewed, especially if we continue to play through the winter months. Traditionalists will no doubt argue that 3pm is perfect but that's no longer the case.

Travelling fans hit too much traffic before and after the match, it often means it's dark by the time they start their homeward journeys, and it impacts on any plans they might have for the evening. Additionally, there is more likelihood that pitches will become frosty during matches as the day becomes darker and clubs face the expense of using floodlights.

There are arguments for the 3pm start. It does allow more travelling time before the match for away supporters and the fact that it's traditional is important; also, some players seem to prefer it. However, an earlier kick-off time for weekend games (with potential for winter/ summer variation) will make getting home from games easier and often safer. Another plus is that it opens up the possibility of pursuing other activities after the match – and with so many demands on people's time these days, this is likely to be welcomed by many fans. Kick-off times should reflect the preferences of supporters at different clubs.

- ✓ fans avoid peak travelling times
- ✓ time for post-match activities
- ✓ safer travelling conditions
- ✓ clubs save on cost of floodlighting

Over-Concentration of Senior Clubs

AMALGAMATION AND GROUND SHARING

Are there too many senior clubs? Probably, but it would take a brave man to try and disband any of them. Supporters' allegiances would be unlikely to transfer to other clubs and the fans would be lost to the game forever. However, the fact remains that the Central Belt is saturated with senior football clubs and other hotspots include Angus. In Dundee, there are two clubs in the same street. There are lessons to be learnt from the amalgamation of two Inverness teams to form Inverness Caledonian Thistle – now well established in the top division. At the least, Dundee and Dundee United could consider sharing a stadium, ideally, purpose-built – what a boost the city would get. While the new stadium was under construction – either on the site of Dens or Tannadice – the clubs could ground-share. A new stadium and a new training centre in the same street – imagine! What are they waiting for, a Russian billionaire? Just get on with it!

For the Central Belt and the rest of Angus the solution is less obvious. Small-town clubs in Angus are unlikely to be in favour of coming together to form a new 'Angus United', and I personally wouldn't like to see that happen, but if push comes to shove amalgamation should be kept in mind as a possibility. Ground sharing isn't always an option but there are many other things that could be shared, such as a regional football centre with training facilities, back office administration tasks, ticketing etc. This is where the football authorities should be taking the lead. With many clubs doing their own thing, there is a lack of consistency regarding many aspects of their operations and while I'm not advocating that every club should be set up in exactly the same way, some clubs do better than others, so why not cherry pick the best models? Youth Football Scotland is an example of what can be made available. Their website is a comprehensive information source on everything from football boots to sports science, and offers excellent guidance for organising a football club.

  ✓ ground sharing makes sound financial sense
  ✓ shared administration tasks save money
  ✓ co-operation will nurture community spirit

Improving the Stadium Experience

MULTI-USE OF FOOTBALL STADIUMS

Stadiums are a key part of the football infrastructure and should be to a good standard. Scottish stadiums, however, are a real mixed bag with some excellent new modern facilities and some crumbling embarrassments. They need to play a bigger part in the clubs and communities as a whole – even some of the modern ones.

The lack of investment has been going on for years and can't be put down to the recent financial crisis. Not only does it show a real lack of respect for the supporters, it's hardly a good advert for the clubs in terms of attracting fans and players.

Why would anyone want to spend an afternoon in a dilapidated stadium with poor facilities? Why would children and teenagers want to put up with an environment like that when they could enjoy some time in a virtual world online? Many of the clubs out there have failed the fans in this respect and some could pay the ultimate price – closure – for not being prepared to invest and maintain their infrastructure.

More imagination is required. Stadiums and associated buildings should be in use every day of the week for business, pleasure and leisure. Too many of them look as if the cobwebs are blown away every other Saturday in the expectation that the faithful mob will trudge in as usual. This is no longer acceptable.

I believe we are now in the 21st century? These days people expect more and, in my experience, are willing to pay more if the quality is better. Simple things like wi-fi, pleasant catering outlets, bars, cafes and shops would make such as difference.

On the positive side, a number of clubs had lots going on in and around their stadiums (this has been flagged up chapter by chapter). And that's the way ahead, to have lots going on around the stadiums with the main arena the jewel in the crown – everything should lead to the main arena, the centrepiece of the local community.

IMPLEMENTING ALL-WEATHER SURFACES

Artificial pitches (3/4G) are becoming more common in Scotland. The pitches look better, are truer and, most importantly in my opinion, create a better footballing ethos because they encourage a more controlled style of play. They are also cheaper to maintain and very seldom are they unplayable.

On my tour of the stadiums, the games I saw played on artificial surfaces were better and teams that played their home matches on them played better football overall. For example, Stenhousemuir v Airdrie at Ochilview Park was a superb game of football played on the deck at a high tempo – great to watch. The quality of performance was undoubtedly related to playing and training regularly on a synthetic surface.

One of the benefits artificial turf has over grass is that the all-weather aspect offers much enhanced multi-usage sports potential – the main pitches at Airdrie and Stenhousemuir are available for hire, thus generating additional revenue for the club. The training centres at Heriot Watt University (Hearts Academy), Murray Park (Rangers) and Lennoxtown (Celtic) all have artificial surfaces and Forfar recently confirmed that they would be installing one. Club Chairman Neill Wilson told the *Forfar Dispatch*:

> This is a unique, pivotal moment for the town of Forfar; it is our opportunity to step forward and say we want our senior football club to lead the way, to be an example of how a club can be the centre of the community, leading and not being led or, even worse, not involved at all.

The idea of using artificial surfaces generates mixed views. In my opinion, especially for the lower leagues, they are a must. They will produce more than just good football: not only the clubs but whole communities will benefit.

REINTRODUCTION OF TERRACING FOR MATCHES AT ALL LEVELS

Terracing works without any problems in the lower leagues and we all stand at Hampden for Scotland games – so what are we waiting for? While I fully understand the move to all-seated stadiums after the disasters at Ibrox and Hillsborough, I am firmly of the belief that we should be able to manage safe standing areas in football grounds.

During the review I stood on numerous occasions and have good memories of the games in Alloa, Brechin and Arbroath – it makes for a much better atmosphere.

Yes, I can remember some moments during the '70s and '80s when standing crowds swayed, sometimes violently. However, improved engineering and control measures should ensure that situations like that are a thing of the past, allowing all clubs to offer fans a choice of viewing options.

Resulting from their recent promotion, Ross County are currently 'upgrading' Victoria Park, to meet SPL standards. That basically means putting seats in standing areas – a complete waste of money in my opinion.

ALCOHOLIC DRINK

The sale of alcohol pre-match, at half time and full time is usually restricted to the hospitality sections. Surely the average supporter should also be able to get a pint before a match?

I love going to Hampden to see the national team play, there are few pleasures like it. It's great to meet up with friends, have a few beers and talk football.

Unfortunately, finding an establishment to enjoy a drink in comfortable surroundings before meandering along to the ground is almost impossible. Hampden is not the only stadium where this is the case, it's much the same at Ibrox and Parkhead and I'm puzzled by the situation.

Why on earth can we not get a pint with our pie? There are few places better policed in the country than football stadiums. Factor in the stewards, CCTV and all the other information available (tickets, supporters clubs' membership lists, electronic data, etc) and you have an environment that is not just well controlled, it's almost auditable. It makes far more sense to serve alcohol in this setting, rather than giving fans no choice other than some dingy, packed boozer where double and treble rounds are the order of the day due to the chaos that ensues on match days.

I understand that as a nation we have a problem with alcohol and that this has to be addressed. So why not encourage orderly social drinking in a well-managed environment, rather than binge drinking in chaotic pubs and clubs?

The authorities need to look at the bigger picture. Lots of people want to drink before football matches and suitable facilities should be provided. If they are not forthcoming, people will continue to throw as much as they can down their throats in as little time as possible, and in reality this only compounds the drink problem in this country.

I managed to take in a game at Arsenal's Emirates Stadium a few seasons ago and was pleasantly surprised to find alcohol on sale inside the ground. The foyer areas were full of fans enjoying a drink and a chat before the game. No drinks were allowed out in the main arena and those who unwittingly tried to venture out with a beer in hand were politely reminded of the policy. I saw no trouble whatsoever. The fans enjoy it, the clubs make some money – this is contemporary football in a civilised manner.

RAISE CATERING STANDARDS

Major changes are required here. Even at the big, modern stadiums the food is usually average, the selection is limited and service varies from reasonable to extremely poor. Yet good quality catering at football matches can only mean extra revenue for both clubs and caterers. I'm really surprised that some of the larger fast food outlets haven't got a foothold in this potentially lucrative market. Again, it comes back to lack of respect for the fans – we deserve better.

We need a Jamie Oliver or a Gordon Ramsay to shake up this tired catering culture. The clubs need to address the male-orientated pie and Bovril mentality – I'm sure more women would come to games if they could get a nice sandwich and a coffee in the stadium.

I've said it before, but people expect more these days and they will spend if the right products are available.

COVERED STADIUMS

In a climate like Scotland's, there is an argument to be made for covered stadiums. Now I'm not suggesting that every stadium is like Wembley, quite the contrary, in fact in the smaller stadiums it might be easier to cover their arenas. Many of the lower league clubs have such small attendances that they could easily be housed indoors, and why not? An indoor arena could be so much more useful than an outdoor one that only gets used every other week. Think of the potential uses and the improved comfort levels for the spectators and players alike.

Initially I thought this idea was 'pie in the sky' but when you look at the regional football centre at Toryglen in Glasgow it suddenly becomes a very real option. Yes, for the bigger clubs it may not be viable unless there is finance in place for a major stadium redevelopment but it's certainly worth a look.

> ✓ place stadiums at the heart of the local community
> ✓ all-weather surfaces encourage a better style of play
> ✓ all-weather surfaces – cost-effective, more reliable than grass
> ✓ year-round multi-sports use
> ✓ terracing makes for a better atmosphere
> ✓ good catering will bring in more people and profit
> ✓ fans will enjoy a pint with their pie

Adding Up the Costs

REDUCED ADMISSION PRICES

At a Second or Third Division game, an individual can spend up to £20 on a ticket plus programme and refreshments, while admission prices for First Division and Premier League games really hits you in the pocket – on average, £30. Reduced admission prices and good deals for families will attract more people and ultimately this would mean more revenue and a better atmosphere at matches.

The introduction of streamlined admission systems and ticketing would reduce overheads and very many clubs need to look at this. All too often I was required to go to a portacabin or ticket office to buy my brief before heading to the turnstile. Combining these two functions – and the purchase of programmes as well – would obviously cut down on burdensome administration and costs. What could be simpler?

Also, offering tailored packages (ticket, refreshments, programme, raffle tickets etc) is something that will help fans know exactly how much their day is going to cost. Interestingly, Raith Rovers recently announced 'substantially reduced prices' for season 2012/13. A club spokesperson said,

> The Board are aware that finances are tight for many families at this time. We are also very keen to attract the next generation of supporters and so primary school pupils can pick up a season ticket absolutely free.

Short-term pain for long-term gain – good on them at the San Starko!

Likewise, the Livi Lions are seeing the light. Now comfortably settled back in the First Division, the West Lothian outfit is promising attractive, attacking football from a pool of exciting young players – at a potential cost of less than £7.00 per game. Great value, they deserve to pack them in next season.

FREE ENTRY FOR CHILDREN

The more children that get the football bug, the more are likely to go to football on a regular basis – and so attracting them is fundamental to the future of the game. The cost of taking kids along to football matches can be extortionate and this needs to be addressed. A few clubs already let kids in free and the SFA recently announced that under 16s would be allowed in for nothing at the Youth International Matches. It's good to see initiatives like these.

CHEAPER PRICES FOR AWAY FANS

Away fans are crucial for the atmosphere at a game – Ibrox and Parkhead are living proof that a lack of away supporters can turn full stadiums into a morgue-like environment.

Why not reduce admission prices for away fans to compensate them for their travelling expenses? Hopefully, this wouldn't be discriminatory to the home fans and if every club did it, maybe more fans would go to away games. I've always preferred away games, the travelling support tend to put much more effort into getting behind their team and it makes for a better day out.

Clubs could appoint away match co-ordinators to provide information on special deals for travelling fans and alternative activities for accompanying family members. Joined-up thinking like this is required for football to prosper.

✓ cut ticket prices
✓ streamline ticketing arrangements
✓ ticket/refreshment packages
✓ kids in free
✓ reduce prices for visiting fans
✓ away match co-ordinators

More Lassies Required

TIME TO ENTICE MORE WOMEN INTO THE GAME

Women are, arguably, football's greatest untapped resource. Has the time come to give them more influence in what can sometimes seem like the last bastion of the male – the beautiful game? Growing numbers of women attend games, but the aim should be to draw more in right across the board.

There are also significant numbers of women players and this is not just a modern phenomenon – Scotland was apparently the first country in the world to encourage women to play football. In the 18th century football was linked to Highland marriage customs – single women would play games against married women and male spectators would sometimes spot their prospective brides – interesting!

Today's women, I assume, are playing and watching the game for enjoyment rather than to impress future partners. Women's football is one of the fastest growing sports in the world. Gabby Logan's programme on sexism in football highlighted that almost one in three supporters attending games in England are female and almost 25 per cent of the TV audience are women. Yet Scottish football is still largely an archetypal male environment. Why not do more to entice half of the population along to games?

If I took my wife out and offered her a pie and Bovril for lunch I'd be wearing it! Throughout my stadium tour, I saw very little to tempt the ladies. Then recently, I came across the Jagettes – could this be the eureka moment? This bunch of female Partick Thistle supporters are trying to bring a bit of glamour to the old game, and what a great idea.

Imagine if every club had a large contingent of female supporters, making a day or evening of it at the football. Ladies Days seem to be catching on – Elgin City have just held their third and as Kate Taylor explained in the SFL newsletter:

> We call it our 'Ascot Day' as we all get dressed up to the nines and make a real day of it. The attendees are all Elgin fans and some of them come along every time there is a home game but this was a way of doing things a bit differently.

Moneymen, take note, there's huge potential in this one.

Not every woman will feel inclined to dress up and head out to Borough Briggs or Recreation Park but for me it's all about broadening the appeal of the game to suit different tastes, and if that means a ladies' section or day, then get it on the agenda and give it a go.

How long will they put up with poor facilities, terrible catering, freezing weather, lack of competition and high prices? These are considerations for us all, whatever our gender, but those of the male persuasion tend to accept the status quo. Maybe it's time to give women a place at the top table.

- ✓ more women in the boardrooms
- ✓ a better range of events at football clubs
- ✓ facilities improved to suit different genders and tastes

Leadership Issues

LEADERSHIP REFORMS

Lack of leadership is a major problem for Scottish football. Year after year our teams crash out of Europe at the early stages. Looking back on seasons 2010/11 and 2011/12 it's the same old story – qualifying round failures, often to teams from so-called 'lesser' leagues and without the European pedigree of our teams.

When is someone going to take the lead and end this embarrassing annual fiasco? For as long as I can remember, European football has been one of the biggest let-downs in the sporting calendar. I relish the prospect of European nights, but most end in abject disillusionment. After the exits there are the usual grumblings but nothing ever seems to happen. Roll on another 12 months, the draws are made and off we go again, full of hope, only to be brought crashing back down to earth by some European minnow. So, SFA, SPL, SFL, whoever, it's time to do something! We need to address this slide into the abyss. The national team has been pretty poor for a while as well with the only highlights coming during the Euro 2008 qualifying campaign. I fully understand that we have no divine right to win or even qualify, but we should put in place the strategies and structures to give us the best possible chance of getting into major tournaments – it's important for Scotland.

Co-ordinated leadership surely means having a single organisation that represents all the stakeholders. Now, whether it's the SFA or SPL or A.N. OTHER, is irrelevant. What is important is that there is consensus on the common goal and that everyone, including the often outrageously critical media, pulls in the same direction. This organisation needs to look at the big picture, taking cognisance of all aspects of football – not just playing the game – the length and breadth of the country. And, it must not be afraid to make radical changes.

There is some good stuff going on. The SFA's Scotland United 2020 Vision sets out a clear strategy, but does this strategy align with the aspirations of the SPL and the SFL? And can they work together for the good of the game? This is the million dollar question. There is much debate about football associations the world over and this will continue until these organisations are more open and accountable. The SFA appear to be moving in the right direction, with significant changes undertaken recently – they were in danger of imploding due to their antiquated culture.

There is also some bad stuff going on. Take the decision to hit Rangers with a 12-month transfer embargo and a fine for bringing the game into disrepute. My view is that this decision is not constructive. For a club with debts alleged to be around the £134 million mark, to be fined £100,000 is absurd. Will they increase it when Rangers don't pay on time? One way of enhancing the likelihood of receiving the payment is for Rangers to generate income by being successful on the park. This is much less likely if they can't sign any players (over 18s) for the next year.

Confused? We all are.

The club were also found guilty of acting in an improper manner/ against the best interests of football – curious! Who exactly is responsible? Rangers' joint administrator Paul Clark, of Duff and Phelps, states:

All of us working on behalf of the club are utterly shocked and dismayed by the draconian sanctions imposed on Rangers...

The reality is that the club is suffering from two decades of reckless, incompetent management by certain individuals and the action the SFA has decided to take compounds the situation, making it even more difficult for the stricken bunch trying their utmost to preserve this great Scottish institution – shocking! We can learn from the Rangers' situation. To have one individual with a controlling interest can be risky (Gretna – remember them?). Having said that, some clubs have managed just fine with this arrangement – St Johnstone and Ross County spring to mind.

FAN BUYOUTS

What about fans running their football clubs? In 2002, Stirling Albion gave it a go and became the first senior league club to be 100 per cent fan-owned. Unfortunately, they are struggling at the foot of Division Two and will be playing in the lowest senior league in Scotland in season 2012/13. Similarly, south of Hadrian's Wall, fan-owned Port Vale are floundering and the supporters are looking to the local council for a bailout. While the intentions are good, success isn't always guaranteed with fan buy-outs.

On the other hand, in Germany many clubs now have a one-member one-vote system and it appears to be working with attendances on the rise year-on-year – encouraging stuff.

Perhaps the answer is to be found in the Community Interest Clubs and societies that are now starting to emerge. Clyde (who are following the German model) and Motherwell are good examples of how to involve the fans and let them get a foothold in the running of their clubs in a sensible, structured manner. These processes are evolving and it will be interesting to see how they develop over the coming years. I wonder if a similar co-operative would work at the SFA?

✓ a common goal
✓ one organisation running the game
✓ Community Interest Clubs
✓ more fan representation at clubs
✓ more fan representation within governing bodies

So is the Baw Burst?

OK, it's going down but all is not lost. We need to think about what we want to achieve and put in place a strategy to realise these goals. If sound business plans are in place to support the sporting strategies, financial security and possibly profit may follow. However, if we let the pursuit of profit dominate all the arguments and become the primary goal, then we might as well forget it.

What we need is an updated vision for the game. The clubs have got to be at the heart of communities and operating in a manner that takes account of the expectations of the 21st-century football fan. They need to be modern businesses that are competitive, useful and efficient that can adapt to an ever-changing society.

The league structures need to be altered to level the playing field. I also believe that the football season needs to change because the game should be played when the weather is better – this will improve the quality of the football, as will the universal introduction of artificial surfaces (which have advantages from a business point of view as well).

I enjoyed the majority of the football matches I saw during season 2010/11 and this season they have also been good. But it can be a struggle getting to the football every week for your average fan, and I wonder if the powers-that-be fully realise this – ticket price and all the other incidental expenses really add up. This is why it is so important to listen to the fans' views, not only regarding costs but also on the future of the game. They are and will continue to be the lifeblood of our national sport and their voices must be heard.

Scottish football has a lot going for it. Loyal fans continue to support their clubs and at many clubs there is decent infrastructure in place. Most importantly, there is huge potential.

Whoever is going to lead us out of the football wilderness could do worse than embark on the journey around the grounds in Scotland. An impartial look at the clubs and the fans over the course of a season is enlightening and I believe that every football-minded person should give it a try – I recommend it.

So, is the baw burst?

Definitely not, but it's time for action.

GET THE DEBATE GOING ON THE BLOG, AT TWITTER OR ON FACEBOOK
HTTP://ISTHEBAWBURST.CO.UK

Also published by Luath Press

Over the Top with the Tartan Army
Andrew McArthur
ISBN 978 0 946487 45 5 PBK £7.99

Thankfully the days of the draft and character-building National Service are no more. In their place, Scotland has witnessed the growth of a new and curious military phenomenon. Grown men bedecked in tartan, yomping across most of the globe, hell-bent on benevolence and ritualistic bevvying. Often chanting a profane mantra about a popular football pundit.

In what noble cause do they serve? Why, football, of course – at least, in theory. Following the ailing fortunes of Scotland isn't easy. But the famous Tartan Army has broken the pain barrier on numerous occasions, emerging as cultural ambassadors for Scotland. Their total dedication to debauchery has spawned stories and legends that could have evaporated in a drunken haze but for the memory of one hardy footsoldier: Andrew McArthur.

Taking us on an erratic world tour, McArthur gives a frighteningly funny insider's eye view of active service with the Tartan Army. Covering campaigns and skirmishes from Euro '92 up to the qualifying drama for France '98 in places such as Moscow, the Faroes, Balarus, Sweden, Monte Carlo, Estonia, Latvia, New York and Finland.

I commend this book to all football supporters... You are left once more feeling slightly proud that these stupid creatures are your own countrymen.
GRAHAM SPIERS

Stramash: Tackling Scotland's Towns and Teams
Daniel Gray
ISBN 978 1906817 66 4 PBK £9.99

Fatigued by bloated big-time football and bored of samey big cities, Daniel Gray went in search of small town Scotland and its teams. Part travelogue, part history, and part mistakenly spilling ketchup on the face of a small child, Stramash takes an uplifting look at the country's nether regions.

Using the excuse of a match to visit places from Dumfries to Dingwall, *Stramash* accomplishes the feats of visiting Dumfries without mentioning Robert Burns, being positive about Cumbernauld and linking Elgin City to Lenin. It is ae fond look at Scotland as you've never seen it before.

... a must-read for every non-Old Firm football fan – and for many Rangers and Celtic supporters too.
DAILY RECORD

There have been previous attempts by authors to explore the off-the-beaten paths of the Scottish football landscape, but Daniel Gray's volume is in another league.
THE SCOTSMAN

A brilliant way to rediscover Scotland.
THE HERALD

I defy anyone to read Stramash *and not fall in love with Scottish football's blessed eccentricities all over again... Funny enough to bring on involuntary, laugh out loud moments.*
THE SCOTTISH FOOTBALL BLOG

Hands on Hearts
Alan Rae with Paul Kiddie
'with a foreword by Craig Levein
ISBN 978 1908373 02 1 HBK £14.99

[Rae] was one of the most trustworthy, wonderful, lunatic, crazy, loveable, straight-jacketed men I have ever met in my life. JOHN ROBERTSON (Hearts striker 1981–98; manager 2004–05)

[Rae] was an absolutely fantastic physio who even though he worked in tiny little physio room at Tynecastle got people back from injury very quickly. A wonderful man with a very dry sense of humour who was brilliant company. SCOTT CRABBE (Hearts midfielder/striker 1986–92)

As Heart of Midlothian FC's physiotherapist, Alan Rae was a vital member of the Tynecastle backroom staff for more than two decades. He was one of the few constants during a tumultuous period in the club's rich history and his behind-the-scenes recollections will fascinate and entertain in equal measure.

From international superstars to mischievous boot-room boys, Rae shares his unique insight into the life of a great Scottish football institution. *Hands on Hearts* is a must-read for football fans everywhere – Jambos or otherwise – and for anyone who has ever wondered about the healing properties of the physio's magic sponge!

Hands on Hearts *is a rich source of anecdotes about the more unusual characters who were on the club's books during the Rae years.* THE SCOTSMAN

100 Favourite Scottish Football Poems
Edited by Alistair Findlay
ISBN 978 1906307 03 5 PBK £7.99

Poems to evoke the roar of the crowd. Poems to evoke the collective groans. Poems to capture the elation. Poems to capture the heartbreak. Poems by fans. Poems by critics. Poems about the highs and lows of Scottish football.

This collection captures the passion Scots feel about football, covering every aspect of the game, from World Cup heartbreak to one-on-ones with the goalie. Feel the thump of the tackle, the thrill of victory and the expectation of supporters.

Become immersed in the emotion and personality of the game as these poems reflect human experience in its sheer diversity of feeling and being.

The collection brings together popular culture with literature, fan with critic, and brings together subject matters as unlikely as the header and philosophy.

[this book] brings home the dramatic and emotional potential that's latent in the beautiful game. THE LIST